THE
TEMPLETON
TOUCH

THE TEMPLETON TOUCH

William Proctor

DOUBLEDAY & COMPANY, INC.

GARDEN CITY, NEW YORK

1983

Library of Congress Cataloging in Publication Data
Proctor, William.
    The Templeton touch.
    1. Templeton, John, 1912–   . 2. Capitalists and
financiers–United States–Biography. 3. Templeton
Foundation–History. 4. Religion–Awards–History.
I. Title.
HG172.T45P76   1983   332.6′092′4 [B]

ISBN: 0-385-18302-X
Library of Congress Catalog Card Number: 82-45873

Contents

Preface

This book contains the authorized account of John Templeton's life and investment philosophy and also the history of the Templeton Foundation Program of Prizes for Progress in Religion. In producing this volume, I have devoted many hours to in-depth conversations with him in a variety of settings, including his estate in the Bahamas, international airplane flights, business and directors meetings, and social gatherings. He has been completely open in sharing his personal insights and techniques and has contributed changes to ensure that his investment philosophy is fairly and accurately represented.

For my part, I have found that even though we differ in our personal beliefs in a number of ways, I have learned a great deal from John Templeton about self-discipline, positive thinking and investment strategies. He is, indeed, a modern-day "sage" on many different levels.

I am also especially grateful to Dan Williams and Todd Moore for their invaluable editorial assistance in helping to do research and pull the diverse threads of this manuscript together.

Finally, I conducted in-person interviews with most of the winners of the Templeton Foundation Prize for Progress in Religion in various parts of the world. So I want to express my thanks to a number of people who were instrumental in making my travels, research and writing a great deal easier.

Rev. Wilbert Forker, Vice President of the Templeton Foundation, was of great assistance in my effort to secure interviews with a number of the prizewinners. Sharry Silvi helped in many ways with the section on Chiara Lubich, such as by serving as translator in Rocca di Pappa, Italy, and contributing a considerable amount of background information. Doug Baker, of the Corrymeela Community in Northern Ireland, was of great assistance in setting up an interview with Mother Teresa of Calcutta.

Brother Émile of the Taizé Community in France provided tremendous help in serving as liaison and interpreter for Brother Roger of Taizé. Professor Jonathan Katz of the Indian Institute Library, Bodleian Library, Oxford University, gave generously of his time in helping me do research on the late Dr. S. Radhakrishnan. And Professor Bimal K. Matilal of Oxford was also quite helpful in providing background information on Dr. Radhakrishnan.

THE
TEMPLETON
TOUCH

1

What Is the Templeton Touch?

Every age produces individuals who possess an extraordinary capacity for acquiring wealth. They seem to have a special gift or "touch" that enables them to accumulate material goods at a rapid rate.

Less successful people—including those who may have great aspirations to "make it big" but have not yet reached real wealth—often wonder: "Do I really have what it takes to reach the top . . . to formulate a personal investment strategy that could secure my family's financial future . . . or even to move beyond mere security and make a fortune?"

A major purpose of this book is to explore, through the life of John Marks Templeton—who may justifiably be called one of "the world's greatest investors"—the question of what it takes to succeed as an investor. Templeton was born into a small-town Tennessee family of limited means, and he and his folks were severely pinched by the Great Depression. Yet this relatively poor southern boy had the seeds of success in his personality, and he nurtured those seeds into full bloom in his adult life as an investment sage.

How did Templeton do it? What is the secret of his success as a "super investor"?

Part of Templeton's formula for material success is very practical: It's been a matter of implementing specific investment techniques which can be learned and applied by almost anyone who possesses a fair amount of desire and persistence. In the ensuing pages we'll see how John Templeton's upbringing was crucial in implanting in him the basic inner drive and personal values necessary to reach the peak of performance as an investor. And we'll also examine in detail—through Templeton's own words and advice—how anyone with adequate motivation can learn his key investment techniques, like bargain-hunting and developing good judgment in selecting stocks.

But there is also another important side to the highest levels of happiness and success in investing—a side that encompasses far broader considerations than just the "nuts and bolts" techniques of accumulating wealth. As we'll see, it's essential to understand and affirm this broader dimension of making big money if you want to be *truly* successful and live happily with your wealth once you acquire it. Too often a person may forge ahead and do quite well in building up his personal assets. But then the unexpected pressures and temptations of his newfound wealth present so many problems that his "success" turns out to be not a success at all, but rather a curse in disguise.

But Templeton has learned how to be comfortable with his riches. He's a self-made man who didn't have the benefit of a family tradition of "old money" and philanthropy, but he has avoided the danger of being "blown away" by his wealth, because he has learned the secret of "successful living with success." Indeed, John Templeton provides one of the best living examples of how a person's wealth can become a satisfying extension of his inner drives and values.

Many of the key ingredients in successful investing are present in the life of John Templeton. He has developed a special "touch" with money which few others even approach. It's a touch that has enabled him to build one of the most successful stock-market investing vehicles in history, the Templeton Growth Fund. And it's also a touch that has inspired him to use the rewards from his investments to promote the moral and spiritual progress of mankind.

But what exactly does this "Templeton Touch" consist of—and how can you make it a part of your own life?

The essential qualities that enable a person like John Templeton or any other successful individual to do exceptionally well in business are undoubtedly dependent to some extent on good genes

—or inherited brain power and other natural bodily endowments. But sometimes success seems to have little to do with innate abilities, as when a person stumbles upon good fortune and then has the ambition and desire to make the best use of his opportunity. In other words, in any great success story there are strong elements of "being at the right place at the right time," and being prepared to act decisively when you find yourself there.

History abounds with tales of various people who were chosen for special tasks and material rewards by God, by the gods, or maybe just by good fortune. But perhaps the most famous story about a special power to create great wealth is the legend of King Midas, the ruler of Phrygia, a large district of Asia Minor in ancient times. There were a number of kings with the name "Midas" who governed Phrygia in the eighth century B.C. But the Midas of ancient mythology probably came from an earlier era—possibly the second millennium B.C., when the Phrygians migrated from Thrace or Macedonia.

According to ancient mythology, on one occasion the legendary Midas encountered the forest god, Silenus, who was a close companion and mentor of Dionysus, the Greek god of wine, fertility and revelry. Silenus wandered drunkenly into Midas' royal gardens, got lost and finally was rescued by the king. Dionysus was so happy when Midas returned his friend that he promised Midas he would grant him anything he wanted. And Midas, a materialistic man, asked for the power to turn everything he touched into gold.

Dionysus agreed and bestowed this gift upon him. But the problem with the "Midas Touch" was that *everything* that the king touched, without exception, turned to gold—including his food and drink. In other words, the touch, valuable as it was, also proved to be fatal.

But Midas was lucky. He went back to Dionysus and asked the god to take away the touch, and Dionysus agreed. He told the king to bathe in a certain stream, and the golden touch disappeared—though the stream continued to be a great source of gold!

A number of interpretations of this story might be offered. But the lesson that seems most appropriate for our present discussion is that even though the king had great powers to create wealth, he almost killed himself because he got caught up in total materi-

alism: He became consumed by an unbridled desire to build up a
store of vast riches without considering the consequences.

Wealth, if it is to be accompanied by true satisfaction and
meaning, must have a purpose that goes beyond mere accumulation. Otherwise, material goods may actually careen out of control, turn on their possessor and eventually destroy him.

If the Midas Touch is one side of the coin of wealth, the Templeton Touch is the other.

You see, the Templeton Touch is, in fact, the opposite of the
Midas Touch. King Midas' ability to produce wealth was a negative force that remained radically self-centered and, as a result,
nearly destroyed him.

In contrast, the Templeton Touch is essentially a positive
power.

First of all, it's a capacity which enables the investor not only to
make a good investment, but also to have more "staying power"
in turning that good investment into a great one. Hard work and
good judgment, supported by self-discipline and patience, are key
qualities that have catapulted John Templeton from being merely
"good" to being "great."

Secondly, the Templeton Touch implies a willingness and an
ability to use one's material gains in some beneficial way for other
people. But this social consciousness of wealth goes beyond mere
"do-goodism" or ordinary philanthropy. In essence, this attitude
involves a sense of stewardship, a belief that what you have is held
in trust for the good of mankind.

Now let's examine the Templeton Touch in more detail by
moving from these general principles to the practical world of
making money. There are several key personal characteristics—at
least fifteen of them—that have helped John Templeton to be regarded by many people as the world's greatest living investor. He
had the seeds of some of these qualities as a child, but none really
came into full flower until his adult life. In other words, he *developed* into a great investor. So his story is a story of personal progress, with success growing gradually until it finally bloomed years
later.

Here is an overview of those fifteen key ingredients in Templeton's personality and some suggestions about how they may relate
to a successful investing strategy.

• *Self-reliance.* From his earliest youth, Templeton was taught to think and act for himself. He developed a belief in himself, a self-assurance and self-confidence. Invariably, this is a crucial quality in the successful investor, who must ultimately stand alone as he makes the final decision about where his money will be placed.

• *Reasonable risk-taking.* Most successful investors—and John Templeton is no exception—seem to have a bit of the entrepreneur in them. But even though Templeton is willing to take adventurous risks with big money, he is, above all, a rational and responsible risk-taker. He carefully analyzes all the factors before he puts even a penny on the line.

• *A sense of stewardship.* This may seem a strange quality to include among those associated with successful investing. But actually, it's one of the most important.

Many outstanding investors, including Templeton, have a feeling that the money they are accumulating represents something of value beyond mere worldly riches, and perhaps even something sacred. This is not to say that they *worship* money. Rather, it's a matter of showing great respect for the potential power of wealth and also gratitude for their ability to earn fortunes. In Templeton's case, this attitude really does approach a sense of stewardship, or an assumption that he has merely been given the privilege of managing assets that have been entrusted to him.

In some ways, Templeton's attitude is true in a purely worldly sense, in that he does manage great sums for others through his mutual funds and the investment accounts that wealthy individual clients have entrusted to him. But there is also a spiritual dimension to his approach because he believes that even his personal assets were given to him by God.

This sense of stewardship encourages great care in making decisions that involve the disposition of money. And it also engenders a deep commitment to thrift—one of John Templeton's most apparent personal characteristics.

• *A drive toward diversity.* The principle of diversity has always been one of the foundations of successful investing: In other words, it's important to spread your risk by putting your funds into a variety of investment vehicles, so that if one has a bad year or goes under, you won't lose all your capital.

But Templeton goes beyond this traditional interpretation of the diversity principle to search *worldwide* for good investments. Many pundits who have tried to explain his success have stressed the fact that his diversity is not merely national, but is international as well.

• *A bargain-hunting mentality.* Searching for bargains is part of John Templeton's basic approach to life: This orientation affects the way he buys furniture, cars—and stocks. Part of his bargain-basement style with stocks involves looking at low price-earnings ratios and other traditional investment techniques. But, as we'll see, his approach is much broader than that taken by most of his fellow investors.

• *A broad social and political awareness.* The present and future value of stocks and other investments is always dependent to some degree on the nature of local social movements, laws and government regulations. Even the basic nature of the political system may have a dramatic effect on how well a given investment will do in future years. For example, Templeton steers clear of investments in countries which are characterized by what he calls "socialization"—or various forms of socialism and other concerted governmental influence in business.

• *Flexibility.* There's no ironclad formula or doctrinaire, rigid rules that guide the top investors. These experts are always willing to "roll with the punches," always flexible when new situations and challenges confront them.

• *A willingness to devote large quantities of time to studying potential investments and developing sound money-making strategies.* This key quality of the best investors may not be particularly glamorous. On the contrary, it is a rather ordinary characteristic. But at the same time, it's an absolutely essential ingredient for investment success. A willingness to work hard for relatively long hours and to do in-depth analyses of specific stocks and investment situations are a *sine qua non* for making profits in this field.

John Templeton doesn't waste many of his free minutes when he travels in airplanes, waits for business appointments, or finds himself in situations which most people would consider "dead" or wasted time: Instead of sitting for minutes or hours staring out into space, he reads articles and studies by security analysts on various companies that interest him. As a result, he is one of the best-prepared investors in the world when it comes to knowing the facts about a variety of potentially profitable opportunities.

• *An ability to "retreat" periodically from daily pressures.* The retreat concept is a religious notion that has direct application to effective investment strategy. Templeton found that when he moved from Wall Street to his present home in the Bahamas in the nineteen-sixties, his success as an investor improved markedly. The hours he spends in solitude help him to get a perspective that was impossible in the hullabaloo of the New York financial markets. These times of reflection also give him the courage to make decisions counter to prevailing market fashions—and often enable him to make money even as the majority of other investors are losing theirs.

• *An ability to develop an extensive friendship network.* One of Templeton's most endearing qualities is his ability to make and keep friends in a wide variety of fields and geographical locations. As it happens, many of these friends are in influential positions in the business and investment community, and they are invaluable contacts when he needs advice or information about a particular investment possibility.

• *Patience.* One of the "fruits of the Spirit" listed in St. Paul's letter to the Galatians (5:22) is patience. And this personal quality is just as important in successful investing as it is in authentic spirituality. John Templeton has learned to be patient and persistent as he selects a certain stock and then waits calmly for it to start an upward climb. The wait may be months or years, but Templeton takes the long view—and his patience has proven him right more often than not.

• *Thought control.* This quality may at first seem rather ominous, because thought control may be associated with control from the outside, as happens in some religious cults or political brainwashing situations. But Templeton's approach to thought control is just the opposite. He advocates and practices imposing, from *within,* a discipline and restraint on the direction of one's thoughts and emotions. In other words, his thought control is really a form of self-control or self-discipline. He has learned, over the years, to focus his mental powers only on the task at hand and to block out all extraneous influences that might distract him from his main purposes in business and life. The result has been an ability to achieve great things in the worlds of investing and philanthropy.

• *Positive thinking.* This is a form of thought control that Templeton practices, but it has a "life of its own" and therefore must be listed as a separate quality. He believes that negative thoughts are a kind of psychological poison that tend to sap a person's energy and distract him from accomplishing his important goals. He certainly recognizes poor or negative investments when he sees them, but he doesn't dwell on them. Instead, he moves on quickly to those investments that offer the positive promise of greater profits.

• *Simplicity.* Although there is a great deal of intricate analysis involved in evaluating many of the companies and special investment situations that Templeton considers every week, a major feature of his investment decisions—and of his entire life, for that matter—is simplicity.

After all the complex elements in an investment decision have been considered, he tries to boil them down to their essential components. But even though the final statement of the solution of a problem may reflect classic simplicity, it still takes a genius of sorts to get to the true essence of an investment problem—just as it took a genius like Einstein to state the simple formula for the Theory of Relativity.

• *Great intuitive powers.* This final key quality for successful investing has an almost mystical aura about it. It's a matter of knowing through some undefinable insight—after all the hard work, risk-taking and other concrete ingredients for a good investment choice have been added—that a certain decision is the right one.

In part, this special intuitive quality may be innate: Some people may naturally be more farsighted and have better judgment and insight than others into what may make a profitable investment. But there's more to it than the right genes. It's also a matter of having laid the groundwork by developing the other fourteen qualities for successful investing. Chances are, if you've acquired these other traits, the intuition and insight will follow.

But Templeton also adds another special ingredient at this point: In short, he seeks to "work in harmony with God's purposes" in that he spends time praying and meditating about the spiritual implications of his investment decisions. He even opens his directors and stockholders meetings with prayer.

Finally, each of these fifteen qualities for a superior investor has a spiritual dimension: They are specific expressions of universal principles that can contribute to a happy and effective life far beyond the business world.

For example, the risk-taking that is necessary for effective investing has its analogue in the spiritual realm as the risk or gamble that the prospective believer takes on God—or the "leap of faith," as some philosophers have described it. Similarly, the sense of stewardship and responsibility that the most effective investors have toward their funds may be likened to the religious belief that the worldly goods we have are not our own, but gifts from God which should be disposed of in accordance with His wishes.

But we'll delve into this connection between material wealth and spiritual principles in more detail later. For now, it's most important to remember that there's much more to becoming a great investor than merely acquiring an intellectual grasp of certain narrow techniques that can be used to make more money.

In the last analysis, becoming a success in the world of investments involves a long-term—perhaps a lifetime—commitment. It's a matter of nurturing and developing essential personal qualities over years and even decades.

2

The Seeds
of Self-reliance

". . . the great man is he who in the midst of the crowd keeps
with perfect sweetness the independence of solitude."
                                        —Ralph Waldo Emerson
                                        "Self-Reliance"

"I'll buy two Roman candles!" said one boy.

"Give me the pinwheels!" cried another.

"A dozen firecrackers for me!" said still another.

Money was changing hands so fast that you might think an experienced adult entrepreneur was at work in this fireworks sale before the Fourth of July.

But such was not the case.

At the ripe old age of eight, John Marks Templeton was the
salesman who had found the market and was raking in the profits.
Even in those early days in his hometown of Winchester, Tennessee, John was already beginning to make his mark in the world of
business. And one of the most striking personal characteristics he
displayed, even as a child, was an ability to formulate an idea, to
plan far ahead, and then to summon up sufficient self-confidence
to *act* on that idea.

In many ways, young John was a personification of that ideal of
inner direction which the consummate American philosopher of
personal independence, Ralph Waldo Emerson, described in his
famous essay "Self-Reliance." In the late eighteen-thirties, Emerson put it like this:

"Trust thyself: every heart vibrates to that iron string. Accept the place the divine providence has found for you. . . . Nothing at last is sacred but the integrity of your own mind. . . . What I must do is all that concerns me, not what the people think. This rule, equally arduous in actual and in intellectual life, may serve for the whole distinction between greatness and meanness. . . ."

Because Emerson is one of his favorite philosophers, John Templeton undoubtedly at some point read those exact words. But even more important, he grew up in a milieu where those basic principles were held in high esteem. The schools, churches and families he knew felt it their duty to teach "strength of character," which meant reliability and self-control. Moreover, unlike many of his playmates, he felt an inner drive virtually from toddlerhood to incorporate those values into his own life in the most practical way.

So it was quite natural, if highly precocious, for him to step apart from the second-grade crowd in tiny Winchester and have the insight and courage to try something entirely new. John knew that the other children liked to shoot off fireworks both at Christmastime and on the Fourth of July. Every elementary-school student knew that. Also, everybody knew that you had to order fireworks by mail because there was no seller in Winchester.

But John went further: He was able to translate his observations into a conclusion that, because there was no fireworks store in his hometown, there was a vacuum in the market—and hence, an opportunity for him.

So John did a little research to see how he could buy quantities of fireworks at cut-rate prices and then sell them at a profit to his classmates. Before long, he discovered a mail-order outlet in Ohio; and soon, about a month in advance of each holiday, he was ordering various kinds of fireworks from Cincinnati through the Brazil Novelty Company's catalog. Roman candles, pinwheels, sparklers, firecrackers—you name it, and he had it. Then, a few days before each holiday, he would pack up his wares into his school satchel, run off to class and sell them to the other children for five times what he had paid for them.

Quite a profit for a kid of eight!

But that was typical of John Templeton. He was always coming up with unusual schemes and planning ahead for ways to put his ideas into effect—especially ideas that would bring in some extra spending money. And these habits and insights, which became part of his personality as a child, stuck with him.

For example, he became aware of the danger of debt at an early age, and by the time he was a teen-ager he had decided that the biggest threat to many families' personal finances was excessive borrowing. So he made a vow, then and there, to be a lender if necessary, but *never* a borrower. And until age forty he never even owned a credit card or a store charge account.

John Templeton, then, was a young man who knew his own mind and had the self-confidence to act boldly on his convictions. In many ways, as his mother had said, he was "born old"—a child with the judgment, reliability, foresight, self-control and many of the other character traits of a wise, seasoned adult.

But where did such a youngster acquire the seeds of self-reliance and the sense of financial responsibility that blossomed so fruitfully later?

No doubt part of his personality makeup came from the role models he observed around his own home. Born on November 29, 1912, the second son of Harvey Maxwell Templeton and Vella Handly Templeton, John grew up in what might be considered, from a city perspective, a poor family. But when compared with the norm of small-town Tennessee communities in the early twentieth century, the Templetons were definitely enterprising.

Quite the "country style" entrepreneur and self-made man himself, John's father was a lawyer by profession—even though he had never gone to college. But in a town of fewer than two thousand people, it wasn't easy to make a living by legal work alone. So he built and operated a cotton gin, which sometimes ginned as many as two thousand bales of cotton in one season. Even though the farmers paid Harvey only two dollars a bale, that was still enough to support the gin—and the Templeton family—throughout the year.

This business later led to a cotton storage venture; to fertilizer retailing; and to profitable speculation on the New York and New Orleans cotton exchanges. Young John often listened intently as his father described the wheeling and dealing that engaged much of the older man's attention each week.

But Harvey Templeton didn't stop there.

He was also an agent for several insurance companies. And he was acutely tuned in to ways he could profit from the rise and fall of the economy in his section of Tennessee: When farms came up for auction because of nonpayment of real estate taxes, he usually attended the auctions and bought a farm if the price was unusually low. His hope in these cases was to resell the farms for a profit at a later date.

Sometimes his entrepreneurial plans worked, and sometimes they didn't. But young John was always watching—and evaluating —his dad's enterprises. John's convictions about the dangers of personal and business debt were reinforced as he saw many farmers losing their land in these auctions. And his natural inclination toward independence and self-reliance gained strength as he saw the excitement and potential profit that accompanied his father's diversified business forays.

By 1925, Harvey Templeton owned six farms, in addition to his cotton gin, legal work and other business activities. Also, by using low-cost surplus lumber and workmen who couldn't find other jobs, he was able to build about two dozen homes on his growing real estate holdings. He then rented them for from two to six dollars a month—not bad in those days when the value of a dollar meant something.

It was ambition and drive like that which eventually provided a relatively good living for the Templeton family. In fact, they were the second family in the county to own both a telephone and an automobile. So even though they might not have been wealthy by the outside world's standards, John grew up feeling that he never lacked a thing. And most important of all, year by year he observed a gradual increase in the family's financial position through his father's hard work and creative business ideas.

But his father was only half the story of the decisive family influences on young John Templeton.

John's mother, Vella, provided a quite different—but equally important—example for John to incorporate into his own personality. First of all, she was very well educated for a woman in those days. She had attended grammar school and high school in Winchester, and then she went on to study mathematics, Greek and Latin for more than seven years at the Winchester Normal College.

After graduation, Vella's brother, Father John Marks, a Roman Catholic convert and Paulist priest, found her a job tutoring children at the Kenedy Ranch, which spread over more than a million acres in Texas. After two years of that adventure, she returned to Winchester and worked for a while as a milliner in a store owned by her brother, Oscar Handly, who later developed the Miller Brothers chain of department stores. Before long, the local "super entrepreneur," Harvey Templeton, began courting Vella, and she married him at what, for those days, was the relatively old age of thirty.

In her own way, Vella had as wide a range of interests as did her husband. Even though she had a good education and loved to play with intellectual concepts, she was drawn to down-to-earth outdoor activities as well. After she was married, she raised chickens, pigs and cows, and she also liked to get her hands dirty in the family garden. Peaches, corn, asparagus, cherries, cabbage and green beans were her specialties—and so the Templeton table never lacked for plenty of fresh vegetables, meat and dairy products. More than two acres were used for vegetables and flowers, and three more for fruits, nuts, chickens, ducks and other animals.

Young John, along with his brother Harvey, Jr., was often underfoot as his mother went about her daily tasks. And it was in this environment that he learned his first major lesson about the principle of profits—at the tender age of four.

He found, first of all, that with a little hard work, he could grow his own beans in his mother's garden at a basic cost of next-to-nothing for the seeds. Then, when they had grown, he would take them to a local country store and sell them for a handsome profit.

The interesting thing is that John came up with this idea all on his own. His mother allowed him the freedom to set up little businesses, but that was where the outside direction and advice ended. Of course, he learned by the examples set by his father, mother, brother and other enterprising adults. But the initiative came from within.

This may seem so extraordinary as to be almost unbelievable— that a youngster would be making profits on a vegetable business at four, and raking in even more money on a relatively complex, wholesale-retail understanding of the seasonable fireworks market at eight.

But consider that Mozart was composing music at age six. So it may not seem quite so incredible that, at a comparable age, one whom many regard as an investment genius could take profitable advantage of the basic capitalistic principle of supply and demand.

Having the opportunity to learn practical business principles at an early age was only part of John Templeton's early training, however. For that knowledge to take root and to influence his later business career in a dramatic way, there had to be more: There had to be some transformation and growth going on *inside* the boy, an internal process of progress which would make an indelible imprint on his character.

This influence, once again, was something his mother provided, but this time in the form of her religious beliefs.

An active member of the local Cumberland Presbyterian congregation, Vella Templeton and her sister, Leila Singleton, John's aunt, literally kept the church alive by raising enough money to pay the salary for a part-time minister. Also, as part of the church's evangelistic outreach, John's mother earned money in various ways for a Christian missionary in China by the name of Gam Sin Qua, who came to be known as "Miss Vella's missionary." Every week, Vella provided luncheons for the local Civitan Club. For many years this activity provided 50 percent of Gam Sin Qua's total missionary expenses in China.

So here young John saw another way of raising money—and most important of all, he was deeply impressed by what money, once earned, could do to *help* others.

He already sensed, as much as a child can, that many problems can develop if you just go after money for its own sake. Money-making for the sake of money-making can certainly mean increased wealth. But it can also mean a lot of headaches as you try to figure out how to keep it after you get it. And if you lose it—as did many of those local farmers who had overextended themselves on their land purchases—that could be more devastating than if you had never acquired any wealth at all.

But there was more to Vella Templeton's spirituality than might first meet the eye. On one level, she was certainly a quite active Presbyterian church elder. On a deeper plane, however, she was totally committed to a movement that had been gaining momentum in the United States in the early part of the twentieth century —the Unity School of Christianity.

We'll see in more detail in a later chapter just how significant an impact these early spiritual influences had on John Templeton. But for now, let's focus on the key qualities for successful investing that he began to acquire from a very young age. Specifically, he learned from his mother and the Unity movement that:

• Material prosperity is a good thing, and should flow naturally from intelligent planning and preparing spiritually and intellectually for success.

• A major key to happiness and success in life is "thought control," or an ability to discipline yourself to focus your mind on those things that are positive and most productive. Physical healing, wealth, inner peace—almost anything is possible if your mental processes are in tune with the great divine principles of the universe.

• He had the power—perhaps something close to divine power— to achieve what he believed he could achieve.

To expand upon this last point, even as a young boy John was given almost total freedom to do anything he thought best: John's father and mother never, to his recollection, gave him any advice whatsoever; and he was never spanked. Furthermore, his mother never even gave him an unqualified "no," regardless of what he wanted to do—with perhaps one exception: Neither John's mother nor his father ever used alcohol or tobacco in any form, and they did not allow it at parties in their home. Otherwise, the sky was pretty much the limit for the Templeton boys.

Now, there is always some risk in this sort of an approach to childrearing. If you never say, "Be careful!" to a youngster, he may get into hot water or even into serious danger. But despite the lack of close supervision, John managed to make it through childhood unscathed—and may well have emerged a stronger person for the sometimes hair-raising adventures he experienced while operating largely on his own.

As a matter of fact, the lack of parental restraint, coupled with a personal conviction that anything is possible, seemed to imbue him with an overpowering sense of self-confidence. The reason for this positive result may have been that Vella Templeton's *laissez-faire* attitude toward her sons John and Harvey, Jr., didn't reflect a lack of concern or love for them. Rather, as the ultimate Unity thinker, she believed that the divine spark in her sons would guide them in the right direction: God, in other words, was capable of bringing them up much more effectively than she could. As John recalls, "She relied on love and continual prayers and providing books and magazines of the 'how-to-do-it' type."

But still, there was reason for some eyebrows in Winchester to be raised occasionally as she put her rather radical, hands-off, childrearing policies into practice.

For example, when John was about ten years old, he and Harvey were very interested in electricity. And he remembers his mother saying to him: "Go ahead and use the attic for your electricity. I've set aside a space for you."

With this brief word of approval, John, his brother and their friends, relying only on what library books they could find, built complex systems of electrical coils, which they used to transform ordinary house current into voltages above ten thousand volts! John and Harvey performed exhibits for the adults, such as drawing out sparks from the coils as long as three inches, and performing other experiments that usually were limited to college students using a well-equipped laboratory with all kinds of safety precautions.

But perhaps even more risky was an incident that occurred when John was only six. It started when he saw one of the older boys shooting a pistol. Fascinated by the weapon, he went to his mother and asked, "Would you please give me a pistol?"

"No, you're too young," she replied. But as was her custom, she didn't stifle his curiosity by leaving him with an absolute no: "But if you still want a pistol when you're eight, I'll give you one."

Two years later, John, never one to forget an opportunity, asked his mother, "Can I have that pistol now?"

"Well, now, wouldn't you rather have a 410-gauge shotgun?" she said.

Because a full-fledged gun seemed much more useful than a mere pistol, John said, "Sure." Soon he was going on all-day hunting trips with his friends, even though he was only a third-grader.

While some might call this sort of thing dangerous permissiveness, others might say it helped plant solid seeds of self-reliance and self-control in the youngster. However that may be, Vella continued to follow a very free childrearing policy, and in the process tried to expose her children to as much of the world as possible.

One summer, for example, when John was twelve, his mother loaded him, his fifteen-year-old brother and a couple of cousins into the car and took them on an extensive two-month trip throughout the Northeast. They traveled about one hundred miles a day, camped out and did their own cooking.

But this was not a parent-controlled vacation. The kids were in charge just as much as Vella Templeton, with each person participating in selecting the routes and activities and setting up the day's campsite.

And even though they had a lot of fun, the trip was by no means merely a relaxed, carefree sort of affair. Every moment was scheduled, and myriads of stimulating sights and experiences were packed into each day. For example, every time they arrived in a big metropolitan area like Washington, New York or Philadelphia, they would hit all the museums—and that meant every room on every floor of every museum.

It was a hectic two months, but such high-powered activity, combined with intensive learning experiences, was what young John learned to expect and love as a boy. And that trip served to set the stage for still another summer adventure a few years later.

When John was sixteen, his mother loaded up the car again—this time with John, Harvey, Jr., and one classmate—and they headed west. Their goal: to see *everything* west of the Mississippi —all the historic sites, national parks, national monuments and the Pacific Ocean. Again, they were gone about two months, and they camped out every night.

This kind of intensive study of one part of the country or one area of knowledge was part of a regular pattern in John's childhood. From the very beginning, he was devoted to long-range, advance planning. He always had some sort of in-depth project going—usually three or four simultaneously. But not all were as dangerous as his experiments with electricity.

For example, there was his butterfly and moth collection. When he was ten, he and his friends were quite interested in collecting those creatures, but with John leading them, they weren't about to do it halfway.

First of all, they researched the habits and preferred foliage of each butterfly and moth they thought they could capture, and they studied each cocoon they found on various plants. Then, when they captured the insect, they often put it into a screen-wire cage along with the proper vegetation and waited for its eggs to be laid.

With this approach, they could all observe the various stages of a moth's development, from egg to caterpillar to cocoon to moth; and they could also get a perfectly formed adult insect for their collection. All they had to do when that perfect moth was born was to asphyxiate it with calcium cyanide as soon as it hatched from the cocoon.

Finally, with this extensive study and research under their belts, they were ready to go into action. First, they found some broomsticks, made wire loops and attached mosquito netting to complete their butterfly nets. Then they caught their prey, and their carefully prepared scenario of harvesting the perfect butterflies and moths moved along like clockwork.

As you can see, even as a ten-year-old, John Templeton never did anything halfheartedly. He had learned from a tender age to research every relevant detail for his projects in order to achieve the best result. His entire childhood, in fact, was characterized by a dizzying barrage of new experiences and new information. Sometimes he and Harvey were drawn to new knowledge simply because they thought it was fun to try new things and be stimulated in new ways. But frequently the things John elected to try or learn had practical, money-making or money-saving implications.

One of the best illustrations of this trait occurred one day when, barely a teen-ager, he was playing with friends in a hay barn about a mile from his house. During the horseplay, he stumbled upon an old, broken-down Ford.

In a flash of insight about what this decrepit vehicle could mean to him and his friends, he approached the farmer who owned the barn and asked, "Do you want to sell that car?"

"I will if you can come up with ten dollars," the farmer said.

So then, all John had to do was go home, withdraw some of his savings, explain the whole situation to his always agreeable mother—and the car was his. As he had expected, all that went easily. But then came the hard part: finding *another* Ford that could be used for parts to get the first one in working order. This second car had to be the same make and model as the first. So John searched all over the county. Finally, thanks to his persistence and his natural knack for bargain-hunting, he did find another Ford. It was in even worse condition than the first one, but like that one too, it was also available for ten dollars.

So now John had a grand total of two old, broken-down Fords. Some people might have jeered that he had wasted his money, even though he was only out twenty dollars. But unbeknownst to them, he had a plan—a plan that he was confident would turn those two old jalopies into one reasonably smooth-running motor vehicle.

With his equipment and parts assembled and tools borrowed from his brother, John and his eighth-grade friends moved on to the next part of their plan: They knew they were energetic and smart enough to learn how to put a car together. So they gathered around those two old cars every day after school and started transferring the parts from one of the vehicles into the other.

If they got stuck in trying to assemble a workable jalopy, they would go down to the local Ford dealer and read his manuals until they understood where they had gone wrong. They also got to know the mechanics around Winchester and picked up important tips to help them complete their project.

After about six months of working in the afternoons and on weekends, they finally got one of the cars to run. You can imagine the cheers that went up when that engine first sputtered, coughed and then began to putter along! Such old autos were started by hand-cranking—not with any "newfangled" self-starters. Surprisingly, this car that John and his friends had rebuilt continued to work for four straight years—long enough to get him and his friends to and from classes and to out-of-town ball games in style until they graduated from high school.

John had recognized a bargain in those two cars, and with his own brains and labor and the help of his friends, he had turned his dream into a reality—for only a twenty-dollar investment.

Part of the inner drive and initiative that John possessed came out in these nonacademic, extracurricular ventures. But these qualities also appeared in his school career—as early as the first grade.

For example, on the very first test he took in the first grade, a little girl named Ruby Silvertooth scored higher than John. Rather precociously, he thought to himself, "Now, why should she get a higher grade than I did? I must not be trying hard enough!"

So he promised himself that he was going to get the highest grade in the class from then on. And when the half-year results came in, John did have an "A"—the highest grade possible—in all his subjects.

When he took his report card home to show his family, his father decided to reinforce John's inner drive toward excellence. He said, "That's great, John, but I'll make a deal with you. Each time you get a card with nothing but A's on it, I'll give you a bale of cotton. But every time you get a card with anything less than all A's—even one item—you'll have to give *me* a bale of cotton. How about it?"

Some parents might think that such a suggestion would put too much pressure to achieve on a young child. But Harvey Templeton apparently knew his son well enough to know what the reaction would be. John loved the idea and was so inspired by it that he insisted the "challenge" between him and his father remain in effect all through high school.

The final result of the contest?

After eleven years, with two grading periods a year, John's father owed him twenty-two bales of cotton. That's right—straight A's all the way through! Young John had elected to rely on himself and his abilities, and he hadn't found himself wanting.

As you might expect, with grades and an inner drive like that, all of John's teachers liked him. In fact, he was so well-thought-of by the faculty that he quickly gained the reputation of being "teacher's pet"—and was called that to his face by the other students.

But John was an inner-directed boy. He marched to a different drummer. So he just smiled at the kidding and laughed along with the jokers, even as he decided that he would sit on the front row in each of his classes, right under the teacher's nose. This may be another way of saying that even at this young age he was a "contrarian," to use an investment term: He always tried to determine which way the great mass of people were heading, and then he would often strike off in an entirely different (and more productive) direction.

But his reason for this practice wasn't just a desire to act counter to the fashions and trends of the moment. He had also found that the closer he was to his teachers, the less likely his mind was to wander off into matters other than his schoolwork. In other words, he found that by positioning himself physically at the front of the class, it was easier to control his thoughts in a beneficial, positive way. And that, as his mother was constantly showing him, was one of the greatest qualities worth cultivating in life.

It's surprising, in a way, that in the midst of all this youthful individuality John still managed to maintain a position of popularity with the other students. In fact, he was their recognized leader in most important activities.

The reason for his dominant position in the student "pecking order" may have been due, in part, to the fact that he was so sure of himself that he projected an unusually relaxed and amiable image to his peers. Or it may have been that he was active in many extracurricular activities—playing football, debating, organizing weekend dances every fortnight for forty or more students in his home, and participating in school plays, to name just a few.

Whatever the reason for his leadership role, the other children seemed to perceive that he was the one who was always right and most worthy to be followed.

If someone was trying to tell a story or convey some information, for instance, the other kids were likely to turn to young Templeton and ask, "Is that true, John?"

Or when his friends lacked something to do, they'd turn to him and ask, "What will we do now, John?"

When he got a question like this, he was never at a loss for an answer or suggestion. For example, in the spring of the year when he was in fifth grade, there wasn't much homework or any other interesting or demanding activity going on in Winchester. So he suggested to his friends, "Come on over to my house—we'll find something to do."

On that occasion, John organized most of the kids his age in town into a new game he had devised called "Knights and Robbers." Everyone who lived south of the middle street in town was a Knight, and everyone who lived on the north side was a Robber. They developed their own code of knighthood, carved wooden swords, and even fought mock battles and locked up the prisoners.

After a couple of months, more than a hundred children in town were playing the game weekly—and John, as the inventor, had the last word in interpreting the rules.

In a somewhat different context, almost the same thing happened after John entered high school in 1926. He had heard about fraternities and how much fun they were; but Winchester had none. So John decided it might be a good idea to start a fraternity—but not before he followed his usual custom of researching his new idea thoroughly before acting upon it.

So he visited his cousin, Oscar Handly, Jr., who attended a prep school about twenty miles away that had fraternities. John found out all he felt he needed to know about how they were organized, and then persuaded his cousin to initiate him into the local chapter of Sigma Phi Omega. Upon his return home, John wrote to the national headquarters of his new fraternity and got a charter to start a chapter in Winchester.

This sort of systematic approach characterized everything young John Templeton attempted, whether the ultimate purpose was fun, or financial or academic achievement. But perhaps the most significant project he undertook in high school—a project that was to have a decisive impact on his future as an investor— was the challenge of gaining admission into Yale College.

It all started with an idea he had when he was quite small, as he listened to adults discussing the merits of different types of education. Yale always seemed to pop up in those conversations as perhaps the best college for both Harvey and John to attend.

John had always been goal-oriented, even from those days when he was earning money selling vegetables and fireworks and getting bales of cotton from earning A's at school. So it was natural for him to begin to think about where he would go to college, even before reaching high school. And Yale became the prize he wanted to capture most of all.

But getting into Yale was no easy task—especially not for a country boy from a tiny town in Tennessee.

For example, one of Yale's entrance prerequisites at that time was four years of mathematics. Winchester High School offered only three. But John was used to challenges like this. He had become a good friend of the high school principal, Fred Knight, so he went to him with the problem. Together, they discovered that the local high school could offer another year of math under Tennessee's current regulations. The only problem was that they had to have at least four students—and of course, one teacher.

John had no difficulty in persuading four of his friends to sign up with him. But somewhat more surprising, he also talked his principal into letting *him*—John—be the teacher! So John worked up a lesson plan and taught the class; and to satisfy the Yale requirement, he took the course himself at the same time, even though he was also doing the teaching. All five students passed the examinations, which were devised and graded by Fred Knight.

But that wasn't the only hurdle a Tennessee country boy had to surmount to make it into Yale. Long before his senior math course, John, the consummate preplanner, had learned that he had to take special college entrance exams to qualify for Yale. In those days there were two ways to do that: You could either wait until the end of your third year in high school and take one comprehensive test that would cover all three years; or you could take an exam for each course after the year that it was completed.

John chose the second option for a very practical reason. He felt that the risk of taking only one exam—and perhaps having a bad day—was simply too great. His ultimate goal of gaining admission to Yale was too important to "put all his chips" on one test. So a month after the end of every school year, beginning as a freshman in high school, he drove to Vanderbilt University to take his annual entrance exams.

But John didn't just go in and take those tests cold, without considerable study beforehand. Even as a high school freshman, he was a complete realist. He knew that the content of Central High courses differed from those taught in the top eastern prep schools, and so he resolved to even the score a bit: He sent away for copies of the entrance exams for several previous years and studied them diligently four hours daily for one month before every trip to Vanderbilt.

As usual, this solid, early preparation paid off for John. He was admitted to Yale's class of 1934 in the fall of 1930, just as the Great Depression was carrying the American economy to its lowest point in history.

Despite the dire outlook for the country in those dark Depression days, John Templeton was not one to become defensive or pessimistic about his own future. His home training and early experiences with life had convinced him that with God all things are possible—that he had every reason to be self-confident and self-reliant, and every reason to expect that he would rise to heights of achievement and prosperity, no matter what he attempted.

A kind of "Templeton Touch" already seemed to be in the making: It appeared that only a good education and the forge of adult experience were needed to imbue young John with his full personal powers.

But dark storm clouds were on the horizon—clouds that might even have the power to shake the confidence of a prodigy who had known only success.

3

The Reasonable Risk-taker

The courage to take a chance on what you believe to be right—
that's one of the essential qualities of the topflight investor. But
how do you develop this capacity? And once you have it, what's
the best way to use it to enhance your chances of success?

Whatever it is that empowers some individuals to assume big
risks—whether it's a strong sense of personal security, high intelligence, restlessness, foolhardiness, or a spirit of adventure—young
John M. Templeton had it in ample supply.

When the time came to choose among colleges, for example, he
could have played it safe and attended Vanderbilt University.
After all, he had been accepted there. It was certainly a good
school, a "name" school—and one very close to home.

But that's just the point. Perhaps it was too convenient and too
protected for John. He wanted something different, an unusual
challenge. And for him, of course, that meant Yale.

It didn't matter that he had never seen the New Haven campus,
nor that he hadn't been to an eastern prep school, nor that he
wouldn't know anyone there. You see, his cumulative grade-point
average at midyear placed him among the top ten members of his
freshman class. For this accomplishment he received an award
from the Yale Club of New York.

Not a bad start for a Tennessee country boy!

But John's achievements made what his father had to tell him all
the more difficult: "I'm sorry, John, but I simply don't have the

money to put up one more dollar toward your college. This business depression is worse than anything we've ever seen."

The news came like a sledgehammer blow to John's aspirations and expectations. But when he began to recover from the initial shock, he realized his father's problems weren't all that unusual. It was the summer of 1931. Times were terrible for *everyone*. Few people had work, and even fewer had money. Optimism was perhaps the scarcest commodity of all. Also, he realized that his father had given him in eighteen years far more than twenty-two bales of cotton. So to help his father in the Great Depression, he gave back the twenty-two bales.

At about this time, John began to question his future possibilities seriously for the first time in his life: "What will I do? Should I drop out of Yale and go to work? What's the *right* thing to do?"

Not easy questions. And for weeks John searched for answers. In effect, he did what he always did when he was planning for the future: He prayed and talked with people. He listened to their advice. He thought about their suggestions and offers—including those of his uncle, Watson G. Templeton, who had said, "John, I can lend you two hundred dollars to get back to Yale if you want to try working your way through." And then he thought some more.

Finally, he decided: With his uncle's two hundred dollars in his pocket and a positive "can do" attitude in his head, he returned to Yale at the end of the summer and prepared to do some scrambling for the necessary funds to finish his education. On his arrival, he immediately went to the college's Bureau of Appointments and told them of his financial predicament. Tales of woe certainly weren't uncommon in those times, and plenty of students did have to drop out of college and try to find full-time work.

But John had an excellent freshman record behind him. As a result, not only did he receive a scholarship, but he got employment from the university as well. He had taken a chance in returning to Yale on his uncle's modest loan. Now, to stack the odds solidly in his favor, he had to invest more of his own effort and sweat into making his gamble pay off.

One lesson he learned during this period was: "Always deliver more than you promise." Another lesson, he said many years later, was that "seeming tragedy can be God's way of educating his children." In particular, the need to earn his own college expenses taught him the meaning of hard work and thrift. John says now that the bad news from his father in 1931 was one of the best things that ever happened to him.

His sophomore and junior years found him working on the college annual, the *Yale Banner and Potpourri,* as well as selling advertising space for the *Yale Record,* the college's version of the *National Lampoon.* By the time his senior year arrived he had risen to the position of chairman of the *Potpourri* and also worked as Senior Aide of Pierson College at Yale—that is, he had the job of finding jobs for other students who were trying to work their way through Yale.

The pay from all these positions added up to a decent income—but, unfortunately, not decent enough. Even with his scholarship, John still had to tap yet another of his money-making resources. And he usually made the most of this resource around a dormitory table late at night:

"I'll call," John said.

"All right, I've got a pair of tens, ace high," another student replied.

"I think three ladies beats that," John answered as he reached for the pot.

Poker was the name of the game. And John was good at it— *really* good.

The fact is, he relied on poker winnings to cover 25 percent of his total college expenses. And despite his awesome reputation as a card player, the games were such fun that there were always plenty of Yale students ready to play. The limit on raises in the games was twenty-five cents, so that no player lost more than a hundred dollars over a year's time.

Risky for a student earning his way through college?

Well, yes and no. While no one can deny that there is always a certain level of risk in poker, it was considerably less risky for John than for most people. Or you might say that, for him, it involved a calculated, reasonable risk.

For one thing, John had been playing poker for money ever since the age of eight. His freedom to engage in card games for pennies was just another aspect of the *laissez-faire* approach to childrearing that his parents followed.

Taught by an older, thirteen-year-old boy, John and some of his other young friends would get together on cold winter nights in a little playhouse behind the Templeton family homestead for penny-ante poker. It was a scene reminiscent of Cézanne's painting "The Card Players," which depicts three old men and a fourth onlooker hunched over a wooden table, intensely concentrating on their hands. In an unconscious caricature of this picture, the children would huddle together underneath a single electric light bulb, shuffling, dealing, betting. Even the chips were there, carved out of wood by the boys themselves. The only things missing were the shot glasses, pipes and cigars.

With experience like that, it's no wonder John knew how to play the game well. He had learned how to keep track of the cards that had been played to increase the odds in his favor. And equally important, he knew how to use psychology effectively—a "must" for winning in poker.

But experience in the game wasn't the only factor that helped John control his risks. He also kept a separate bank account for his winnings and losses. The object of this precaution was to protect himself financially—to provide a sort of cushion, if you will, against losses. Any winnings accumulating over the one-hundred-dollar mark automatically went into his expense budget and weren't available for poker.

So, even though playing poker to pay for tuition was a risky venture, it was a risk that John felt he had to take. And it was also a risk that he knew he could handle fairly safely in light of his personal knowledge and proven experience with the game. Later, at age twenty-four, John gave up poker and has not played since. In fact, he never invests in shares of companies in the gambling business, because he has seen so many people harmed by compulsive gambling.

But how to juggle a variety of jobs and how to gamble for fun and profit weren't, by any means, the only things John learned at Yale. Even more important, it was at college that he learned his precious, lifelong habit of time management. When grades have to be maintained to keep a scholarship, every minute counts. And John learned a number of ways to avoid wasting a single second.

For example, he carried papers, books and homework around with him everywhere he went. Anyone who saw him on campus would find him reading, writing, or otherwise studying whenever a free moment appeared in his busy schedule.

If he got to class a few minutes early he wouldn't just sit and stare out the window. Instead, he would pull out a textbook, a half-finished essay or another assignment he needed to complete and go to work for the short time available. And those minutes here and there added up so that he was able to accomplish much more than his peers in the same amount of available time.

But while John never stopped working fifteen hours a day, six days a week, he usually managed to get his seven hours of sleep a night. That, to him, was mandatory in order to keep his energy levels high and do his best work. In some respects, his approach to life, even at that young age, already matched the method of time and energy management discovered by the hardworking founder of Methodism, John Wesley. At age eighty-five, Wesley wrote in his *Journal:*

"I this day enter on my eighty-fifth year; and what cause have I to praise God, as for a thousand spiritual blessings, so for bodily blessings also! . . . To what cause can I impute this, that I am as I am? First, doubtless, to the power of God, fitting me for the work to which I am called, as long as He pleases to continue me therein; and, next, subordinately to this, to the prayers of His children.

"May we not impute it as inferior means,

"1. To my constant exercise and change of air?

"2. To my never having lost a night's sleep, sick or well, at land or at sea, since I was born?

"3. To my having slept at command so that whenever I feel myself almost worn out I call it and it comes, day or night?

"4. To my having constantly, for about sixty years, risen at four in the morning?

"5. To my constant preaching at five in the morning, for above fifty years?

"6. To my having had so little pain in my life; and so little sorrow, or anxious care?"

John Wesley was obviously a prodigious worker who labored from dawn to dusk, but who had the self-discipline to be sure he got enough sleep. And Wesley, through his spiritual resources, also managed to maintain an emotional equilibrium, which further preserved his personal energy in the midst of his frenetic schedule.

John Templeton had embarked on a similar path, with work crammed into every niche of his waking day. And like Wesley, he possessed a positive, success-oriented, stress-conquering frame of mind, though in Templeton's case it had been inculcated in him from his family background rather than from a dramatic conversion experience. Also like Wesley, Templeton learned at an early age that regular sleep, rest and relaxation were absolutely essential for him to keep up a high level of performance in all his tasks.

So even if at first it might sound as though John Templeton was a classic workaholic, he wasn't. His commitment to hard work and his drive toward excellence were balanced by an ability to pace himself with adequate rest. And as part of his capacity to relax—and to maintain good relationships with his friends, as he had learned to do in Winchester—he maintained quite an active social life. His motto was, "Work first, play later." With a wide circle of friends, he attended all the college football games, the big dances and various fraternity functions. He was an active member of Zeta Psi fraternity and Elihu senior society.

Finally, and perhaps most important of all, the extra energy that John conserved from keeping well organized and in good physical and emotional condition, enabled him to evaluate those decisions about his future which involved some risk.

Of course, many of these were the same decisions that all college students have to make—what sort of graduate school, if any, to attend; and what career to follow. But John learned that the best way to make those decisions—and to assume the risks and anxieties that any given decision presented—was to do what he had always been accustomed to do when setting out on a new venture. First, he researched the project or goal he was considering. Then, when he had made adequate preparations, he *acted immediately*. He knew intuitively that the risks and energy-draining worries accompanying any new course of action multiply if (1) you are poorly prepared, or (2) you delay too long before acting on a decision you feel is correct.

Very early in his college career, John saw that there were two or three major goals that he needed to set and strive toward: He needed to do well at Yale and get a degree that would help him as much as possible in the future; he needed to settle on an appropriate career; and he needed to make some decisions about graduate school.

By the time his senior year was completed, his goals had all been achieved:

• He had earned a degree in economics and stood near the top of his class academically, serving as president of the Yale chapter of Phi Beta Kappa.

• He had made a definite decision to become an investment counselor.

• He had set aside three hundred dollars from poker winnings to open his first brokerage account at Greene and Ladd, where his roommate, Jack Greene, was a partner.

• He had been awarded a Rhodes scholarship to study law at Oxford.

All of these developments fit neatly into John's plans for the future—even though he didn't know exactly what the future might hold. It was always possible, of course, that it would be best for him *not* to become an investment counselor. Or perhaps it would be frivolous and even a waste of his time to attend Oxford for two years in the middle of a worldwide depression, when most other people were scrambling around for decent jobs.

Some students then, as now, become immobilized by the pros and cons involved in the wide variety of such choices they must make. But not John Templeton. He knew that, to some degree, all of life is a gamble. No one can ever see every ramification of a given decision beforehand, no matter how thoroughly he plans and prepares. And at a very early age he also learned that it was far better to make a relatively fast decision—a fast "roll of the dice"—and keep moving than to postpone the answering of important questions and allow random events to make those decisions for you.

So, with hardly a look backward, John made up his mind and plunged ahead—his first stop being England and Oxford.

He chose to study law at Oxford for a reason that fit into his emerging plan for his life: He wanted to prepare himself as thoroughly as possible to deal with the various tax and legal dimensions of the investment-counseling business, his chosen future occupation.

But unlike his experience at Yale, John found he had much more free time on his hands. The important change in his status was that there was plenty of money from his scholarship to allow him to get along without working. So instead of spending all his extra time making money, he devoted his free hours to traveling and cultivating friendships that would stand him in good stead throughout his life.

During the first Christmas six-week holiday, for example, he and his Rhodes-scholar friends "did Spain," and on the following six-week Easter holiday they toured Italy. They first bought tickets for unlimited travel on the country's railway system at a very low price. Then they traveled extensively throughout the country, visiting galleries, museums, cathedrals and other major points of interest. They tried to see every place that had two or more stars in Baedeker's guidebook.

In some ways, John's approach to travel was similar to what he had learned traveling as a youngster with his mother, brother and cousins: Educational intensity and thoroughness—along with a variety of new adventures—were the things that made a trip most fun for a Templeton.

During this period one of John's early personal traits—the respect he had developed for the value of a dollar—became even more pronounced. He had always been thrifty and conscientious about good financial planning. And now, even with the extra money he had from the Rhodes scholarship, he was still devoted to this principle.

For example, every trip he took was done on the tightest of budgets. He and his friends developed a system where, upon arriving at the train station in a foreign village or city, they would bargain in sign language with the hotel porters who met the train. Then they would trot off with the one who offered the lowest hotel rate, regardless of how good or bad the accommodations were.

You might have thought that someone with a small-town Tennessee background—even one who had done well at Yale—would be reluctant to thrust himself forward in planning these trips and meeting new people whose language he didn't even know. But not John.

And he showed the same boldness and self-confidence when it came to meeting some of the finer families of Britain through a program called "Ryderising." This was a system of travel in England set up by Lady Frances Ryder to expose American students to proper British families.

Almost from the day of their arrival, her successor, Miss Macdonald of the Isles, would invite them over and say, "Now, as long as you're at Oxford, if you want to visit around the country, just let me know at least two weeks ahead of time. I'll arrange it so that you can choose any location you want for a night or a fortnight—the seashore, London, country estates in hunting areas, or whatever. Just write me."

Some students were too shy and too unsure of themselves to take advantage of this offer. Others just lacked the initiative, for one reason or another. But John didn't hesitate.

He immediately joined the program, and, as a result, met many distinguished British families, including some royalty. In fact, he became so enamored of the British and their ethics and character that he continued to keep in touch with his British friends—and eventually moved to a British colony, the Bahamas, and became a British citizen.

But that's getting ahead of our story. For now, it's important to understand that, for reasons John sensed subconsciously, the personal contacts he was making and the experiences he was having would later be invaluable to him. So he overcame whatever timidity he might have felt, and threw himself enthusiastically into a variety of strange experiences and personal encounters.

Once again, of course, there was some personal risk involved. He might have committed some *faux pas* in these rarefied social circles and been put down or laughed at. The risk of rejection that any outsider runs is rather high in such circumstances. But in John's mind the rewards far outweighed any possible risk. And the more personal successes he achieved in this new environment, the more confident he grew.

But then, upon his graduation from Oxford, he completely shifted gears once more and set out in an entirely new—and much more physically hazardous—direction. He and a close friend, James Inksetter, decided to take a seven-month trip on a shoestring budget through twenty-seven nations, many of them with unstable social and political systems.

Now, it may not seem so unusual for a couple of young men to take a round-the-world trip before they settle down into their chosen careers. But for someone as goal-oriented as John Templeton, who knew precisely what he wanted to do with his life at that time, a seven-month delay in looking for a job during a major depression may seem somewhat foolhardy.

But John knew what he was doing—and his decision to take off and travel for such a long period at this point fitted rather nicely into his career plans. He knew that it would take some time to find the right job, including some weeks or even months to contact companies, set up interviews, and make final decisions when and if job offers came through.

So he decided to take a major step toward finding a job *before* he left on his trip. Then he would have a head start when he returned to the States. Specifically, he made a list of one hundred companies where he felt he could best learn the business of investment counseling. Then he wrote the most persuasive letter he could draft to describe exactly what his background was and what he wanted to do. Finally, he mailed a personalized copy of this letter to his chosen firms and asked for appointments on his return to the United States.

The result? John found, after returning from his trip, that he had twelve appointments lined up. Considering that it was 1937 and jobs were still hard to come by, he felt he had done rather well. Planning ahead once again reaped its reward.

But there were moments on his round-the-world odyssey when he wasn't entirely sure he would even be able to return to the relatively safe and comfortable American environment.

John Templeton and James Inksetter chose to make their trip on a combined total of two hundred English pounds—not much to travel and live on, even in those days. Most of John's share of the pot came from a poker profit of ninety English pounds that he had accumulated at Oxford.

It's true, of course, that he had several hundred dollars in a brokerage account back in the States. But to use that money for consumer spending would have run counter to an investment philosophy he had been developing. As he often told his friends, "If you put aside money for capital, don't start spending it—that defeats your investment plan."

Following his own advice, then, he deliberately chose to travel around the world on a pauper's budget for a full seven months. Their maximum expense for a night's lodging for two was seventy-five cents in Berlin, and the minimum was ten cents in Hangchow. They averaged only twenty-five cents per night for two hundred nights.

How did they manage to stretch their money over twenty-seven countries and seven months? Basically, by planning ahead.

Before they started the trip, they divided the money and mailed it to themselves in five different locations throughout Europe and Asia. This way, not only did they force themselves to live within their budget, but they also protected themselves against robbery and were forced to establish a basic travel itinerary.

Their first stop was Berlin, for the 1936 Olympic Games. And their baggage was as light as their funds: They carried handmade backpacks, bedrolls, one spare shirt each, one change of underwear and socks, four guidebooks, a camera—and a Bible. The choice of a Bible was interesting because at that point in his life John, by his own admission, wasn't a very religious person. Even so, he always worked on self-improvement and used the long hours on boats and railways to gain a good knowledge of all the books of the Bible.

Their experience in Germany was a political eye-opener. The Nazi party was quite strong there at the time, and every morning they heard a rousing chorus of *"Sieg heil! Sieg heil! Sieg heil!"* for ten solid minutes as Hitler entered the Olympic stadium in Berlin.

Some foreigners got very disturbed, even afraid, at these demonstrations of mass hysteria. But John's reaction to the Nazis was not one of fear, but rather of curiosity. This reflected his now well-developed habit of greeting each new situation as an educational rather than a threatening experience. He even made a game out of picking Nazis out of the crowds: He was especially struck by their distinctive, piercing looks and overly serious attitudes toward life.

After five days of Nazi Germany, the young men headed for Yugoslavia to visit a former college friend, then rode the Danube steamer to Bucharest. And it was at this point that things started to get rough.

Their problems began when they misread the train schedule, thinking the daily train to Varna, Bulgaria, left at 10 P.M. rather than 10 A.M. They had carefully spent all their Romanian money before walking to the station. So they went across the street near the Bucharest train station to sleep in the park for the night.

Unfortunately, their choice of outdoor "hotel" made them look more like vagrants than anything else. In a few hours the local police appeared and were asking them what they were doing—in a language they couldn't understand.

The upshot was that they were hauled away to the police station and had to sleep the rest of the night in a flea-infested cell. When they awoke the next morning, thousands of fleas were crawling over them, and they seemed to have at least as many flea bites.

Some people might have given up at that point and gone home. But not these two adventurers. Picking the fleas off each other as thoroughly as they could, they left for Varna the following morning and continued on their schedule, though they were a little the worse for wear.

But so far their troubles were mere child's play compared with what was to come. Perhaps the most disturbing incident occurred where they least expected problems—the Holy Land.

Both young men were in high spirits when they rode the old bus from Cairo to Haifa (then a part of Palestine). The Bible now became an invaluable guidebook. Because they both had first names that came directly out of the New Testament, they began to study all they could about the disciples James and John. And as they read the various stories, they decided that they had to do what those two disciples had done—go fishing in the Sea of Galilee.

Their intentions were admirable. But the experience itself almost cost John Templeton his life.

When they arrived in the Galilee region, the innkeeper at the place where they were staying in Tiberias told them there was bad feeling between the Arabs, English and Jews in the area. So he warned them to be careful and not go too far into the untamed wilderness.

But the two students had their hearts set on fishing the Sea, as the early disciples had done. So John, after a little searching, found a young Arab boy who had learned to speak some English. Through a combination of words and gestures, he asked the boy to arrange a fishing expedition for them for one hour or less, and the boy soon got some Arab fishermen to agree to take the Oxford and Cambridge graduates out onto the water to catch fish.

But by now James Inksetter was having second thoughts: "It looks a little foolhardy," he said.

John, on the other hand, wasn't about to be dissuaded: "We'll never get another chance like this. I'm going, even if I have to do it alone."

And so he did.

All by himself, John climbed into a small rowboat with three Arabs, none of whom spoke a single word of English. They set out around four o'clock in the afternoon, and to his surprise they were still rowing at seven o'clock. By eight o'clock, night had fallen, and they found themselves skirting the opposite shore, which was entirely in the hands of a nomadic tribe of Bedouin Arabs.

John, of course, had no idea where they were or what his guides' plans were. But he began to get a little concerned when they headed for the shore, grounded the boat and motioned for him to get out. Everyone then climbed up a small hill to what appeared to be a Bedouin campsite, and there the Arabs prepared a dish of ground coffee beans. Then, after going through what seemed a short, formal ceremony of some sort with John, they all shared in sipping and eating the grounds.

Needless to say, the repast wasn't particularly tasty. In fact, it was downright repulsive, and John has never been a coffee drinker anyway. But he decided there seemed to be more involved here than just nourishment, so he chose to endure the beans rather than risk offending his hosts.

After he had finished the snack and his stomach had settled down, John finally began to relax a little. But then, all of a sudden, several Arabs appeared out of nowhere and started running toward the fishing party, shouting and brandishing clubs and knives.

As they got closer, it became evident that *John* was the one they were after.

Unknown to him at the time, the little coffee-grounds ceremony he had just participated in saved his life. The three Arabs and their families with whom he had just eaten were now sworn by Bedouin custom to defend him with their lives. And fight for him they did. The struggle lasted about fifteen or twenty minutes, with one side prevailing for a while, and then the other seeming to gain the advantage. Miraculously, no one was killed, though some sharp blows found their marks.

Neither group seemed to really want to annihilate the other, but the attacking Arabs made it clear that they would refuse to leave until John could prove to their satisfaction that he was neither Jewish nor English. Finally, through a combination of sign language and showing them his passport and other documents he was carrying, he satisfied them that he was an American. At that point the gang left as quickly as they had arrived, and John and his three friendly Arabs were free to start back across the Sea of Galilee.

By this time it was two o'clock in the morning, and all John was really interested in was setting his eyes once more on James and laying his weary head on his bed in the inn where they were staying. But the Arabs insisted on fishing on the way back, and John joined in to pacify them. This was not the time to rile up any more Arabs, he decided. They caught about forty St. Peter's fish by the gills in their net and gave the best one to John.

All in all, that was one fishing trip John would never forget. His primary feeling was gratitude that he was still alive. And his mother in Tennessee was especially happy to learn that he was all right, because she had dreamed that he had died.

John also realized that even though risk-taking could be an exciting pursuit, he would have to be more careful in the future about his choice of gambles. It obviously didn't make any sense to take a chance just for the sake of the excitement involved—especially if there was a substantial likelihood that he, or those who were relying on him, might get seriously hurt in the risk-taking process.

So when John finally arrived back in the States after a journey that took him through India, China and Japan, he had managed to learn the life-styles and attitudes of dozens of varieties of people and was ready to settle down and do some serious work in his chosen career. Also, he was a much wiser young man for his travel experiences—and he was something of an expert on how to live happily on ten shillings a day.

In particular, he had a better grasp of the grass-roots economies and practical political systems of a wide variety of countries around the world. The fascination he developed for social and business pursuits in other lands would stay with him throughout his career and have a major impact on his decision to search the world for investment bargains.

Also, John had a better idea now as to which risks in life were worth taking, and which were not. This was an extremely valuable lesson for a person who aspired to become an expert in the heady world of high-risk common-stock investments.

But when he arrived in New York, which he had chosen as his temporary career base because it is the center of investment information, John abandoned his wandering ways for the time being. He and Judith Dudley Folk, daughter of Mr. and Mrs. Rean Estes Folk of Nashville and a graduate of Wellesley College, were married in April 1937. Soon after their wedding, they went to New York for the twelve job interviews that resulted from the letters he had mailed before he went on his world trip. Two solid job offers came through.

Surprisingly, he took the *lower*-paying job, which was a position at Fenner & Beane, a stock brokerage firm which just three months earlier had established its investment-counseling division with only two men, Alpheus Beane and Richard Platt. But John determined that he could learn the most there, even though the position paid only one hundred and fifty dollars a month. His wife found a job as an advertising copywriter at the same salary, and they conscientiously saved fifty cents out of each dollar to invest for the future.

As it happened, though, he stayed with Fenner & Beane only three months. The reason for the short stay was that a fellow Rhodes scholar, George McGhee, who was working in Dallas for a seismograph exploration company called National Geophysical Company, had told his boss about John. The boss, William Salvatori, was so impressed that he made John an offer to come to Dallas as secretary-treasurer of the company for five hundred dollars a month.

But John was never one to burn his bridges. Even though he

decided immediately that he wanted to accept the new offer, he made it a point to talk it over thoroughly with the owners of Fenner & Beane. They had been fair and helpful to him, and he knew he would probably have professional contacts with them in the future.

As he had expected, they agreed that the Dallas offer was too good an opportunity to turn down. So John and his bride headed for Texas and his new job—and it was this position that provided the springboard that launched him on his successful, independent career as an investment counselor.

He worked very hard at his new job and was in almost every respect the model employee: He got to work before his boss whenever possible; he used any free time he had to study business literature that related to the company's work; and he educated himself in accounting and United States tax law.

But his ultimate goal was to have his own business. He never lost sight of that objective, and the opportunity finally appeared. About two years after he had started with National Geophysical, John had a big idea: He reasoned that since war had just broken out in Europe, there was a good chance that many companies which were victims of the Depression would bounce back in a wartime economy. The United States wasn't in the war yet. But John knew from his broad reading that this country would be supplying the Allies and that we would most likely get involved in a direct way ourselves in the not-too-distant future.

Translating these broad conclusions about the economy into practical reality, he decided, in September 1939, to buy one hundred dollars' worth of every stock on the stock exchanges that was selling for no more than a dollar per share. To finance the venture he borrowed ten thousand dollars from his boss.

But it's important to note at this point something further about Templeton's approach to debt. Borrowing money for personal expenses or opening a charge account were taboo for him. But this case was different because it involved a business venture in which the borrowed funds would be used to make money.

In other words, if he had borrowed only for *consumer* purposes —say, to buy a home appliance or a car—the value of the object that he had purchased would inevitably have depreciated. As a result, he would have been stuck with a debt to repay and no chance to make enough money on his purchase to cover the debt. But in borrowing for *business* purposes, he was gambling that the profit from his investment would greatly exceed the principal and interest he would be paying on the ten-thousand-dollar debt to his boss. Incidentally, this was the only time in his entire career that he ever borrowed, even for business purposes.

There were two other factors that reduced the risk in the investment he was making. First of all, he had done thorough research during the previous two years on the performance of stocks selling for less than one dollar. And he had found that if their past records continued, it would be very unlikely that he would lose money. Secondly, through other wise investments and a stock-purchase plan he had with his company, his personal investment portfolio was now worth more than thirty thousand dollars. So there were enough assets to cover the ten thousand dollars he had borrowed in case his theory should prove wrong.

With this analysis in mind, then, he asked his first boss—Dick Platt of Fenner & Beane—to place the order.

"We're going ahead with this unusual order, John, but thirty-seven of the companies you want are in bankruptcy," Platt warned him.

"That doesn't matter," Templeton replied. "Buy everything, whether it's in bankruptcy or not."

Many might call this a high-risk move—especially when you're gambling with your boss's money. But as usual, John had done his homework well. He knew there was a chance that his scheme might fail, but he also knew that he had gathered all the information and analyzed it as thoroughly as anyone could. In other words, he was ready to take a risk, but it was a *reasonable* risk—one in which the odds had been stacked as much as possible in his favor through solid prior preparation.

So the Templeton style for chance-taking in business was a curious—but highly successful—mixture of caution and speculation. And it's perhaps symbolic of his approach that, even today as he puts big money on the line in new investment ventures, he usually wears both a belt and suspenders to hold his pants up. His personal motto is, "OPM is sacred." "OPM," of course, is "other people's money."

As far as the ten-thousand-dollar investment of his boss's

money was concerned, the final reward turned out to be well worth the risk. Out of the one hundred and four companies whose stock he had bought, only four turned out to be worthless. Within a year young Templeton was able to pay back all the money he had borrowed. After he had sold all the stocks, on an average of four years after he had bought them, his original ten thousand dollars had grown to forty thousand dollars.

But Templeton still had made a solid profit. Now he was in a position to strike out on his own—and to develop the Templeton Touch to its full potential.

4

Total Commitment: The Key Requirement for a Great Investor

The slim, polite boy stopped in front of the next house, took a deep breath, put on a positive air and, with hardly a moment's hesitation, walked up and knocked on the door. "I'm giving away a great cookbook, and I'm wondering if you'd like to take a look at it?" he said just as the unsmiling woman opened the door a crack.

She didn't strike him as an impulsive shopper. There was definitely an air of businesslike efficiency about her and her home. But like many of the other prospective customers young John Templeton had approached in this way, she obviously had trouble turning her back on a free offer.

So she opened her screen door, took the book and flipped through it for a few moments. "This *is* a nice cookbook," she said.

"Sure is, ma'am," said Templeton. "And like I said, it's yours free—when you subscribe to *Good Housekeeping* magazine. Here, let me show you these samples."

It was the summer before Templeton went to Yale. And yes, he was selling magazines door to door. And he hated it.

Few people had money in 1930 to buy anything—much less "extras" like magazines. For that reason alone, selling magazines required more than just a "hard sell"—it required all the skills of persuasion and all the perseverance and patience you had. The sales supervisors even told the salesmen to *run* from house to house so they would seem breathless and excited when they approached a prospect—just to make the impact greater.

In Templeton's view, it wasn't too pleasant a summer job. But still, he did well. The company's policy was to give each salesman one dollar for each two-dollar subscription. And if a salesman happened to last through the entire summer *and* hit the two-hundred-or-more subscription mark, he would receive an *additional* two hundred dollars over and above his commissions.

Templeton made it. He stuck it out for the entire summer— unlike many of the others—and he also earned an extra two hundred dollars for his Yale expenses.

What's the moral of this little story?

First of all, Templeton disliked the job. He didn't feel he was the greatest salesman, and he thought the high-pressure methods were not beneficial to the customer or the salesman. But he needed money for school, and the money the job offered was better than any other opportunities he had. So he decided to take the job, and, most important of all, he threw himself wholeheartedly into the challenge.

It was these two factors—a *decision* to act and a *total commitment* to see that decision through to a successful completion—that characterized his approach to business and investing from the very beginning. In this case it wasn't that he felt he had to be the top magazine salesman for *Good Housekeeping*. But Templeton knew that once he had decided to do this sort of work for the summer, he had to do his best. That meant giving it his all, finishing what he had started, and being willing to make sacrifices if necessary to achieve his goals.

Total commitment is the *sine qua non* for success in any phase of business. But to understand the role this important attitude has played in John Templeton's success as an investor requires us to take a closer look at his career development. And as we put his earlier life under our biographical "microscope," at least four distinct "building blocks," which have become the foundation for the Templeton Touch investment method, emerge.

Building Block 1: The ultimate goal. From the outset Templeton sensed the overriding importance of goal-setting in his life. He was never without goals—whether it was building up a fireworks business as an elementary-school student, getting into Yale, or becoming an investment counselor. He seemed to know intuitively that if he merely lived day by day, with no vision for the future, he would drift aimlessly and likely achieve little.

So all the hard work and self-discipline that he displayed, even as a child, always had an ultimate purpose, an ultimate goal behind it. He worked with a plan in mind at his childhood jobs: He wanted to prove to himself that he could be successful as well as generate extra spending money to reduce the family expenses for his father. He continued to work hard, both academically and in his various part-time jobs at Yale. But again, it wasn't work for the sake of work. Rather, he had an important two-pronged purpose in mind: He wanted to do his best in his studies; and he wanted to ensure that he would have the financial wherewithal to support himself at school so that he would be in a position to do his best. The goals were always there; the effort and self-discipline were only a means to that end.

The same considerations applied when Templeton made his decision to go into the investment-counseling business. He first evaluated his own interests and abilities in a thoroughly rational fashion. Then he concluded that there were three reasons why he should become a professional investor:

First of all, he felt that his strongest talent was that of judgment. In other words, he had discovered from his previous experience in life that he possessed a superior ability to weigh the various factors that go into making a decision and then to determine promptly when one thing is better than another. He had an intuitive ability to detect the strengths and weaknesses of varied business opportunities, and also the courage and self-confidence to act on his insights. And of course, this gift of judgment is the very foundation of investment counseling: A financial adviser must be able to weigh all the elements of an investment opportunity and then choose those that will ultimately control the value of the stock or other property in the future.

The second reason why he chose investment counseling as a career was related to the first: He believed that he could achieve greater success and make more money in this field than in any other. And there was a corollary consideration as well. Templeton felt that as an investment counselor he would learn a great deal about other fields of business. As a result, if it became hard or impossible for him to make a living in his chosen field, he could transfer relatively easily to another line of work.

The third reason why Templeton picked investment counseling eventually became the most important: He felt that in this type of work he could help people. In a sense, he saw this field as almost a public-service occupation, because he had the opportunity to help families at many different income levels save money and even acquire wealth and security.

As John Templeton launched his career, these three reasons became intertwined and virtually indistinguishable as he moved steadily toward his ultimate goal—the highest level of success as an investor. But even though an ultimate goal was fixed in his long-range vision, he refused to dwell on it or to fall into the fallacy of "living in the future." Rather, he shifted his gaze to the daily tasks at hand—the tasks that would finally pave the way, step by step, to great success.

So, from the outset, the service-oriented John Templeton spent hours in research, in study, and in getting to know the personal qualities of management teams of various industries. Yet he always did a bit more with his clients than most other investment counselors. He especially believed that those who relied on him deserved personalized treatment, including a complete investment program designed for their *specific* needs and requests. In short, a personal touch became an integral part of the Templeton Touch.

"I always tried to please everyone with whom I came in contact," he said, "including all clients and employees."

As an example of this trait, he notes: "We now have more than two hundred thousand investors in our mutual funds, and I have managed dozens of businesses for more than forty-five years. But I have never been sued by anyone—nor have I ever sued anyone."

In fact, Templeton has never even been in a courtroom as a witness. It's been said, "You can't build a fortune or a great corporation without making enemies somewhere along the way." Plenty of people may disagree with him on any given topic. But so far as he knows, nowhere in the world does John Templeton have a real enemy.

This philosophy of treating people well has also carried over to his attitude toward his employees. Templeton is known as a man who saves and cuts his expenses to the bone. But he doesn't skimp when it comes to hiring top talent. "I believe the best bargains in executives and employees are found by paying about twenty percent more than the salaries available elsewhere," he says. "In other words, a truly able employee is worth more than two mediocre employees. Therefore, it's a wise policy to pay unusually generous salaries to attract the highest quality associates."

Other than hiring well-qualified workers and treating each client as a special individual, Templeton, from the outset of his career, avoided any pat formulas for putting together an investment portfolio. He decided precisely how much *each* of his clients should have in bonds, stocks or other property. And he offered a complete estate and financial planning service, with an emphasis not only on appreciation of investments but also on the reduction of income and estate taxes. Each person had slightly different investment goals, such as imminent retirement, education of children or accumulating enough capital to invest in a new business enterprise. And just as Templeton stressed the importance of having ultimate goals in his own life, he also recognized the significance of such goals for others—and tried to tailor their portfolios and programs accordingly.

Building Block 2: The doctrine of the extra ounce. Because of his attentive and conscientious service, Templeton's business prospered. And once the operation started to grow and needed additional office space, he moved the research division close to his home in Englewood, New Jersey. This way, after dinner with the family, he could go back to the office in the evenings. Also, the proximity of his office to his home made it easier for him to work on Saturdays and Sundays and thus enabled him to provide even better service for his clients.

But a question that will immediately come to the mind of many people is this: Was all this work really necessary for him to reach the top as an investor and build a great fortune? He had a wife and before long was the father of three children—and he found himself spending increasingly long periods of time away from them to attend to the affairs of his clients. Was such sacrifice really necessary to achieve the heights of success? Was it best for his family in the long run?

Templeton always thought it was. And his conviction about this aspect of total commitment to his work and his career goals arose from a philosophy he began to follow when he was a child in Tennessee. As a boy, he observed people a great deal, both young and old alike. He would watch them in every phase of their lives, study them, and question why they did certain things—and what impact those things had on their happiness and levels of success. One thing that particularly intrigued him was the discovery that people who were *moderately* successful did *almost* as much work as those who were outstandingly successful. The difference in effort was quite small—only an "extra ounce." But the results in terms of accomplishment were often dramatic.

Templeton called this principle the "Doctrine of the Extra Ounce." And he quickly noticed that the doctrine was not confined to just one field of endeavor but applied in all fields. In fact, it seemed to be a kind of universal principle that could lead to success and great accomplishment in life.

For example, when it came to high school football games, Templeton discovered that it was the boys who tried a *little* harder and practiced a *little* more who became the stars, or at least contributed the key plays that won the games. These boys tended to be the ones who got the cheers from the fans and the compliments from the coaches. And all because they did just a *little* bit more than their teammates.

Templeton also noticed this very same Doctrine of the Extra Ounce at work in his high school classrooms. Those who did their lessons reasonably well received good grades. But those who did their lessons a little bit better than anyone else—who exerted that "extra ounce"—received top grades and all the honors.

The same principle applied to his experience at Yale. Templeton made sure that he had his lessons not just 95 percent right, but 99 percent right. The result wasn't just getting into Phi Beta Kappa his senior year: It was getting into it during his *junior* year and being elected president of the Yale chapter—an accomplishment that went a long way toward helping him be selected for a Rhodes scholarship.

It's no wonder, then, that Templeton ran his investment-counseling business the way he did. In his opinion, the one who did good work could expect a comfortable life. But the one who did a *little* better than that could expect a fortune.

And that's the way it worked out for Templeton. He did indeed amass a fortune. But the Doctrine of the Extra Ounce was only one among several important factors that was at work. At the same time he was putting in that little bit of extra effort, he was freeing maximum amounts of his personal cash for investment by following a life-style that literally served as a definition for the word "thrift."

Building Block 3: Thrift. When John Templeton and his wife Dudley got married, they pledged to love, honor and obey, just like everyone else. But they also pledged to set aside 50 percent of their total earnings for a personal investment portfolio.

For a full understanding of such commitment to thrift, it's helpful to take a look, once more, at the Tennessee boy's childhood. In his hometown of Winchester, a person's honor and character were all-important. And one of the major marks of solid character was thrift. A person who didn't save something—at least a few dollars out of his weekly paycheck—was regarded as undisciplined. Or, as the town gossips put it in those days, he was "shiftless."

In contrast, being thrifty was a sign of self-respect and self-reliance. So, right from the beginning, young John Templeton learned that thrift was a character trait worth developing. And after the crash of 1929 and the advent of the Great Depression, the importance of thrift became even more apparent. There was ample evidence on the streets of the nineteen-thirties to reinforce the notion that saving as much of your money as possible and investing it wisely are essential to security and success. Quite simply, those who practiced thrift received great rewards, and those who didn't suffered much more from financial setbacks and economic uncertainties.

So young Templeton stuck by his decision to set aside fifty cents of every dollar earned. But it wasn't an easy decision to carry out—not by any means. That kind of thrift required total commitment—the kind of commitment that is an integral part of the Templeton Touch.

To make the personal sacrifices a little more tolerable in the early years, they even made a game out of being thrifty. And friends and neighbors often helped in the couple's radical personal financial venture.

For example, acquaintances discovered restaurants where they could get a full meal for fifty cents. They usually tried to keep the cost under fifty cents because that amount was approaching what they considered expensive.

Furthermore, Templeton never paid more than a hundred dollars a month for rent—*never!* The fact is, he set a goal that rent would never be more than 16 percent of annual "spendable income," defined as the money left over after taxes, savings and investments. But he became so adept at finding bargain-basement housing that rarely was that percentage even approached.

The Templeton approach to apartments obviously excluded living on Park Avenue or in any other affluent section of New York City. But they didn't need luxury. They could get along without it, and get along without it they did, in almost every other imaginable area of life.

When it came to furniture, for example, the first few apartments were already furnished, so they didn't have to worry about decorating or buying. Then, when they finally did rent an unfurnished apartment and started buying things, the decor was still in bargain-basement style.

As a matter of fact, they furnished a five-room apartment for only twenty-five dollars. This feat—incredible even for the hard-pressed nineteen-thirties—was accomplished by going to auctions and bidding on pieces of second-hand furniture when no one else offered a competing bid. As a result, at one auction Templeton got a bed for a dollar and a sofa for five dollars, and he managed to furnish the entire apartment for a pittance.

Anything not available at auctions or flea markets, John Templeton himself constructed out of wooden boxes. The result, of course, was not the most elegant apartment in town. As one wag observed, " 'Early attic' was the basic style of the place!"

But their various abodes during the early years were warm, homey and acceptable because of their shared long-term goals. Their great thriftiness was more an adventure than a burden, as they believed deeply in what they were doing. They had a definite objective toward which they were saving—total financial security—and they knew the near-poverty conditions under which they sometimes seemed to be living wouldn't last forever.

Of course, the irony of Templeton's style of life was that he wasn't poor at all. In fact, he had a good income and a strong, steadily growing investment portfolio. Some acquaintances might have regarded his approach to money, housing and the conveniences of life as somewhat eccentric, if not socially unacceptable. After all, the circles that Templeton, the investment counselor, ran in were characterized by big money, big houses, big cars and sometimes big consumer spending in general. In the minds of many of his business colleagues and clients, there were right places to live, right restaurants to go to, and other right ways to spend your money.

But John Templeton wasn't one to live by rules formulated by other people. Certainly, he was a personable young fellow, liked and respected by almost everyone. He didn't go out of his way to alienate people, but at the same time he had definite ideas about how he should live his life. The drummer he marched to wasn't about to skip a beat because someone, for no good reason, said that a particular practice or habit of Templeton's was unacceptable.

So a radical philosophy of thrift became a deeply rooted part of the Templeton way of life. And in a development closely related to this thriftiness, he acquired a profound aversion to personal debt.

Building Block 4: No consumer debt. As has been mentioned earlier, John Templeton at a very young age decided that he never wanted to borrow money to cover his ordinary consumer expenditures. In fact, he made an *absolute* commitment never to borrow for nonbusiness purposes, never to own a credit card, and never in any way to get himself into debt.

A major reason for his opposition to debt was that he had seen as a youngster what borrowing had done to many families: It had strapped them financially and almost made them prisoners of those from whom they borrowed.

For example, Templeton always remembered a particular workman whom he knew as a child in Winchester. The man worked six days a week for a dollar a day. But consistently the workman went to another Winchester worker in the middle of the week and said, "I can't wait until Saturday for my six dollars. I need some money right now. If you'll lend me five dollars, I'll pay you back six on Saturday."

Naturally, the other worker always agreed to this offer. Who wouldn't? This loan amounted to 20 percent interest for only three days—or 2,420 percent interest per year!

Even though John was only in the eighth grade at the time, he realized that the borrower was paying that excessively high interest and always coming up short in his personal finances simply because he lacked financial self-discipline. He fell into this kind of borrowing because he failed to take the time and exert the effort to set up a simple personal budget.

Observing this sort of real-life, grass-roots economics lesson in Winchester wasn't Templeton's only education in the use and misuse of money. He also read and studied the lives of Benjamin Franklin and John D. Rockefeller and other biographies. And he took to heart what Rockefeller said about wealth: If you want to become really wealthy, you must have your money work for you. The amount you get paid for your personal effort is relatively small compared with the amount you can earn by having your money make money.

These ideas fascinated John—so much so that he would spend time in his room studying compound-interest tables for hours. He always enjoyed mental arithmetic games: He even figured out how much the Indians would have made if they had taken the twenty-four dollars in trinkets they had received in 1626 from the Dutch for Manhattan Island and invested it at 8 percent annual interest. According to his calculations, they would have had $240 billion by 1926, or sixty times as much money as the U.S. Federal budget in that year. This meant they would have been able to buy Manhattan back for $15 million per acre—and still have billions left over!

When he got older, the principles relating to debt that he had learned as a child stuck with him. In a rather radical departure from normal homeowning practice, he bought his first home entirely with cash. These days, most people would argue that a homeowner should always take out a mortgage so that he can shelter part of his income from taxes through deductions of the mortgage interest. Also, common financial wisdom says that it's a good idea to keep as much of your capital as possible free from being tied up in a home so that you can use it for other investment purposes.

But John Templeton has never been one to go along unquestioningly with the common wisdom. He always felt that having a home subject to a mortgage put the average person in the undesirable position of being deeply indebted to someone else for perhaps the most important material possession in the world—the shelter for one's family. What if the homeowner should lose his job, or encounter especially bad times in his business so that his income dropped dramatically? In that event, all the tax deductions on mortgage interest in the world wouldn't do much good if you didn't have the money to make those monthly mortgage payments. Without an adequate income, you'd end up not with mortgage interest deductions, but with a mortgage foreclosure—and no place at all to call home.

So Templeton, not one to formulate ivory-tower theories that he himself fails to apply, bought his first home with cash. Located in Englewood, New Jersey, the house was twenty-five years old and was built on three quarters of an acre. While it was valued then at approximately twenty-five thousand dollars—the amount that would have been necessary to rebuild it from the ground up— Templeton bought it in 1944 for only five thousand. The bargain-hunter *par excellence* had struck again!

As it happened, despite the extremely low price, Templeton was quite satisfied with this new home, and he lived there for a number of years. The merits of his approach to house-hunting soon became apparent. Not having any monthly mortgage payments naturally made it possible to accumulate more money for investing. And because Templeton had picked his home and neighborhood wisely, the house increased in value all the years he lived there. Eventually, he was able to sell it for $17,000 and then buy a bigger home in a better neighborhood for the same price they had obtained for the old one.

So once again Templeton was able to avoid a mortgage, buy his second home outright, maintain the security of his family's shelter and uphold his personal philosophy of avoiding all consumer debt.

But how would Templeton feel if he were looking to buy a home today? Would he advocate purchasing a place with cash only and no mortgage?

The answer is yes, he would do the same thing again, if it were at all possible to do so with the current high price of houses in many parts of the country. And even if he couldn't buy the house outright, he would never subject himself to a mortgage equal to more than half a year's income.

For example, if a person's income is fifty thousand dollars a year, Templeton believes that person's mortgage should not exceed twenty-five thousand. The reason for this guideline is that if something goes wrong in some other aspect of the individual's personal finances—say, some tragedy like a physical disability or getting fired from a job—there would be some chance that mortgage payments could be met or the mortgage paid off entirely. Disability payments, for instance, might cover the relatively small mortgage payments. Or a severance payment following the loss of a job might be enough to cover the remainder of a small mortgage and at least ensure that the family had shelter, if nothing else.

Now, as has already been noted, many financial experts might argue these points—especially from the tax standpoint. They would argue that an intelligent, well-educated person like Templeton or his peers should never worry about where the next paycheck is coming from. The key point, they would say, is that the bigger the mortgage, the bigger the tax write-off.

In Templeton's opinion, though, staying out of debt puts you in a much better position to make big money than does lowering your taxes. Therefore, the benefit of having a smaller mortgage with less debt will significantly outweigh a bigger mortgage with greater tax deductions.

But Templeton's resistance to paying interest was not limited to big purchases, like a home. He has always been just as concerned about finding bargains among the smaller consumer items and then buying those items outright, with cash on the barrelhead.

Take automobiles, for instance. He spent less than two hundred dollars for each of his first five cars. His reasoning was simple: Unlike many friends, who were paying anywhere from a thousand to five thousand dollars for new autos, Templeton figured that all he needed was a car that ran reasonably smoothly—not some "showmobile" that would only depreciate in value. His style was always to put his big money on assets that would increase in value, not decrease.

And this approach to cars applied equally to all other forms of transportation. He always used the cheapest means of getting around that he could find. On his trip around the world, you'll recall, he and James Inksetter always traveled by the lowest class available. And today Templeton still chooses coach class in the air, and public transit, such as subways and buses, on the ground.

These, then, are the four major building blocks that have made up the Templeton approach to total commitment as an investor. First, he set a firm goal—to be a great investor and investment counselor. Without this vision, no significant achievement would have been possible. Second, he always put in just a little more effort in studying and analyzing his stocks than anyone else—he always put in that "extra ounce."

Third, he developed a radical philosophy of thrift so that he could free as much of his money as possible to invest and build up his own personal fortune. And fourth, he made his own financial base secure—in fact, virtually impregnable—by avoiding all consumer debt. It's important to note, with respect to this last point, however, that he does often buy shares of public companies which borrow judiciously to finance the purchase of investment properties that may appreciate in value during inflation and thereby accelerate the growth of the corporation's capital base.

But these four building blocks, which constitute the basic foundation for a total commitment to successful investing, are only the first step. After the commitment must come aggressive action— buying, selling and trading stocks, bonds and other investment properties in the risky environment of the world's most high-powered markets.

Now let's turn to the arena of financial combat, where the hasty and ill-prepared are quickly unhorsed and the skillful and most expert ride to financial victory and the ultimate reward of great wealth. It's in this arena that John Marks Templeton wields investment techniques with the same aplomb and virtuosity that the most formidable Medieval knight displayed in brandishing his broadsword or mace.

5

The Bargain-hunting Principle

Many investors have a rather haphazard way of building their portfolios. They may act when they get a hot tip from their broker or when they hear about a good deal from their father-in-law. Sometimes they pull out their checkbooks when they overhear a remark by a wealthy neighbor at a cocktail party. Or because their friends are buying computer stocks, they do too, for fear of missing out.

The result, more often than not, is that they *do* miss out. The stocks rarely seem to go up, and if they should happen to move higher, they're back down as fast as they went up. All in all, their portfolio just doesn't seem to appreciate, or at least not in any meaningful way that rewards them for the risk.

If this sounds all too discouragingly familiar, perhaps it's time to take a look at the Templeton Touch technique of choosing investments. This approach is probably more methodical than what many people are used to. It's also much more time-consuming. Yet the Templeton Touch is far more rewarding too. As evidence of this fact, consider for a moment what Templeton has managed to do during the past two or three decades with the crown jewel of his investment vehicles, the Templeton Growth Fund.

John Templeton started the Templeton Growth Fund back in November 1954, and the achievements of this common-stock mutual fund have been phenomenal. To illustrate, suppose you had invested $10,000 in the fund on January 1, 1962, and left it there

for the twenty years ending on December 31, 1981, with all capital distributions and dividends reinvested in the fund. In that case,
your original investment would have increased to $163,090—and
achieved an average annual rate of return of 15 percent!

According to *Johnson's Investment Company Charts 1982,*
which has tabulated this information, you would have been a
shareholder in the most successful public mutual fund registered
for sale in the United States or any other nation, so far as we
know. Also, it's interesting to compare the performance of the
Templeton Growth Fund with that of the Dow Jones Industrial
Average, which showed only a 5.2 percent annualized rate of return for the same twenty-year period.

The same sort of superior performance record for the Templeton Growth Fund emerges when a twenty-five-year period is considered. The *Johnson's* report shows that a $10,000 investment
would have grown to $309,013, for a 14.7 percent average annual
rate of return.

John Templeton, who has masterminded all the successful investment decisions of the fund, is also fond of displaying charts
that go back to the very beginning of the fund in late 1954. A
$10,000 investment at that point would have dropped immediately
to an actual net asset value of $9,150 after sales commissions
were deducted. But it would then have soared to $364,495 by Oc-
tober 31, 1982, if dividends and capital gains distributions had
been reinvested.

It's worth noting that during that same period of time, the cost
of living in the United States would have caused the buying power
of that initial $10,000 to increase to only $36,632. In other
words, an investment in the Templeton Growth Fund would have
increased by almost ten times the cost of living during the period
in question.

In 1974 Templeton sold to John Galbraith the international
distributing corporation for his funds. Under Galbraith's guidance,
the number of shareholders that Templeton serves has increased
to more than 232,000, with total investments of about $1.7 bil-
lion. Some of these shareholders have invested in the Templeton
Growth Fund, and others participate in two other funds Templeton and Galbraith established.

In 1978 they set up the Templeton World Fund, Inc., and in

1981 they originated the Templeton Global Fund, Inc. It's interesting to note that for the period from 1978 to 1982 the Templeton World Fund had an even better investment record than the Templeton Growth Fund; and that from 1981 to 1982 the Templeton Global Fund had a better investment record than *either* the Templeton Growth Fund or the Templeton World Fund! So it seems that the Templeton Touch continues to have a significant impact on a variety of investment vehicles.

Other Templeton family companies, including the Templeton Investment Counsel, Inc., owned by Templeton's son, Dr. John M. Templeton, Jr., and Tom L. Hansberger, manage a half billion dollars in additional investments for private clients.

John Templeton, then, is clearly a leader of the pack among the active money managers. So it's not surprising that he is consistently mentioned as one of the outstanding investors in history. In a *Financial World* article entitled "The Great Investors of the 20th Century," for example, he is named as one of the three "latter-day investors who number among the greats."

There is no doubt about the magnitude of Templeton's achievements. But the question still remains: What is the secret of his success?

To answer this question, it's necessary to analyze his approach to investing under four distinct headings: (1) the bargain-hunting principle; (2) "broad business principles"—those corporate, social and political principles that guide his decision-making on national and global levels; (3) some very personal principles which are extremely important to his success but not always easy to define; and (4) a set of intuitive or spiritual factors that are perhaps most influential of all in giving the Templeton Touch its distinctive character.

Principle One: Bargain-hunting
"Looking for a good investment is nothing more than looking for a good bargain."
—John M. Templeton

Bargain-hunting has always been a way of life for John Templeton—and that's been especially true when it comes to the stock market. By Templeton's definition, a stock is a bargain if, and only if, its true value is greater than its selling price. Such bargain stocks, in his opinion, are the only kind anyone should buy. Templeton has *never* violated this principle, even when he was just getting started as an investor.

For example, when Templeton bought every stock that was selling for $1.00 a share or less, he considered each one of them a bargain. And that was particularly true of a stock called Missouri Pacific preferred.

This stock had originally been offered to the public at $100 a share and had paid dividends of $7.00 a share. At the time Templeton bought it, the railroad had been in bankruptcy for several years and the preferred shares were available for $.12 apiece. But he figured that since war had just broken out in Europe, railroad traffic was bound to increase. The result, Templeton believed, would be that Missouri Pacific would most likely make a comeback, with shares rising to $2.00 or $3.00 a share.

In other words, Templeton perceived that the shares were worth several dollars, even though they were priced at just $.12. In this case, by the way, the worth of the stock was determined by a number of factors, including the value of the railroad's assets, the impact of the war, and the future need for railway service. "Worth" tends to be a rather fluid term in Templeton's view, the factors that comprise it varying from one company to the next, depending on the value of a company's products or services in a given economic setting.

The final result of this "Missouri Pacific purchase" was a typical Templeton investment tale. In less than two years the railroad company made a comeback. The stock went up to $2.00, then $3.00, and then $5.00 a share—at which point Templeton sold. The shares kept on climbing in value, however, and finally reached a high of more than $100 a share.

By selling the stock at $5.00, Templeton made quite a healthy profit on it. In fact, he received forty times what he had originally paid for it.

But why did he sell out so early? Why didn't he hang on so that he would have a shot at that top value of $100 a share?

The first and most obvious response to this question is that he didn't have the benefit of our hindsight: As good as he is, he can't see into the future and predict exactly when a stock will hit a high or a low.

From his perspective, when the stock hit $5.00 he felt that at that price the risk on the "downside" was as great as the potential rewards on the "upside." In other words, it seemed as likely that the stock might retreat from that $5.00 price as that it might move significantly above it. So it was no longer the bargain it had been at $.12. Also, Templeton had his eye on other stocks which seemed better buys than Missouri Pacific at the $5.00 price. It's also interesting to note that in appreciating from $5.00 to $100, the stock increased twenty times, or only half of its previous performance.

In this particular instance, he freely admits that, in light of what we now know about the movement of that stock, he did sell too soon. But at the same time he points out, "No one ever gets in at the bottom or gets out at the top. The idea is to buy whatever is cheapest. Then, when it has gone up enough so that something else is cheaper, you should sell the first stock and shift to the second."

But many people often wonder, "How can you tell when one stock is cheaper than another?"

Templeton has to respond to this question many times each month in his own work. The guideline he uses goes like this:

If you own one stock and are considering switching to a second, the second stock should be at least 50 percent more valuable than the first one for the switch to be worthwhile.

For example, let's say there are two stocks you have determined, through extensive research and security analysis, to have a true value of $100 a share. The one you own is selling at $40, and the one you are considering is going for $30. Should you switch from the $40 to the $30 stock?

In this instance, Templeton would say no. It's true that both are bargain stocks, selling at less than their estimated value, and the $30 stock is a better buy. But it's not sufficiently so for Templeton to give the green light to buy it.

The percentage difference between the value of the two stocks can be found first by subtracting from the market price of the first ($40), that of the second ($30). The difference ($10) would then be divided by the price of the second stock ($30) to get the percentage by which the second stock is more valuable—or a better bargain—than the first. In this case the $30 stock would be only

33⅓ percent "better," and thus would not meet the criterion for purchase.

Templeton would advise you to stay with the $40 stock until the $30 stock declines to a price that makes it a 50 percent better bargain. In this case the price would have to go below $26 for it to qualify. Or, to carry through the calculations, you would subtract from the price of the first stock ($40), the new price of the second stock ($26) to get $14. Then, you would divide this $14 difference by the price of the second stock ($26) to get the percentage—54 percent—by which the second stock is now a better bargain than the first. Templeton believes that switching from the first to the second stock would be worthwhile probably as often as two thirds of the time in such transactions, when the second stock becomes a 50 percent better bargain.

When is a stock a bargain in the first place? Is there a systematic method or formula for determining a stock's true value or worth?

Templeton's basic formula is to divide the total value of a company by the number of shares the company has distributed. This calculation will give you the *true* value of the company's stock, and if the market price is lower, then it's a bargain.

In some cases this figure can be determined rather simply. With mutual funds, for example, you can take all the stocks of other companies which the fund holds, add up the listed market value for each stock, and then divide the total by the number of mutual fund shares that have been distributed. The answer to this simple mathematical procedure will be the net asset value of one share of the mutual fund. Newspapers print daily under "Mutual Funds" the net asset value of each fund, which is computed in this way.

Some other industries, such as insurance, can occasionally be evaluated in a somewhat similar way. At one point, for instance, Templeton decided that he liked the Yasuda Fire and Marine Insurance Company in Japan. He came to this conclusion after he took all the investments they owned, added up the listed market prices of those investments, and then divided this sum by the number of Yasuda shares outstanding. As a result, he discovered that the shares were priced 80 percent below their liquidating value. Now, that was a bargain, according to Templeton.

But many companies and other investment opportunities can't be evaluated in such a straightforward way. Most require considerably more research and, most important of all, a keen—even artistic—form of personal judgment. Every company and industry has its own special quirks and individual characteristics that must be taken into consideration.

Like many savvy investors, if Templeton is evaluating retailing companies, for example, he looks to see the extent to which the geographical area is changing; the number and character of the people moving in and out of the vicinity; the nature of the company's competition; and the stability and competence of the management. And this is only the beginning. The more information Templeton collects about a specific company or industry, the better he is prepared, he feels, to make a final decision.

So he tends to fill all his "dead time"—the minutes and hours he spends on airplanes and buses, or waiting for appointments—with a sheaf of reports, graphs and analyses on various companies and managers. He reads, studies and weighs the pros and cons of each potential investment in light of these mountains of information. And then he decides. Only in this way can he have the confidence that he is using his personal gift of good judgment wisely, effectively and accurately.

When Templeton is checking up on oil and gas companies, the wealth of information is still of prime importance. But the specifics are different from the specifics for a retail store chain. For oil and gas, he concentrates on the company's cash flow. Cash flow provides more reliable comparisons between oil producers because reported net profits are distorted by many arbitrary choices regarding accounting methods and exploration programs.

Each industry and company, then, has its own requirements when it comes to determining worth and bargains. When evaluating grocery chains, Templeton looks at net earnings. With mining companies he collects information on the ore bodies to estimate how long it will be before the minerals are depleted. The key point underlying his bargain-hunting methods is that his system of evaluating stocks is dependent on extensive research and sound judgment. There really is no easy formula that can be applied across the board to find a good investment value.

Finally, here are some very current tips that Templeton offers to those investors who plan to launch their own bargain-hunting expeditions in the present economic climate:

• The United States is now one of the best grounds for bargain-hunting. But don't misunderstand: This advice from Templeton is not part of some patriotic, buy-American plan. Right now he just happens to think that many of today's American blue chip stocks are worth much more than what they are selling for.

• Although many people think that collectibles are good bargains in this economy, Templeton thinks they are not. Many collectibles are up two, five, and sometimes ten times the prices twenty years ago. And such increased prices are certainly not characteristic of a bargain. So some collectibles may provide a *small* amount of insurance to their owners in this economy, but most are not really attractive investment opportunities at present.

• If you want to find a bargain, look for *unpopular* investments —not those that are on everyone else's "buy" list. "If you buy the same stocks that other people buy, you'll have the same record as other people," Templeton says. "The only way you can hope to have a record superior to other people is to buy what the other people are not buying."

In many cases, buying unpopular stocks requires you to look for trouble: In other words, it's important not to shy away from a company just because it's currently having problems. Temporary troubles can signal a major bargain-hunting opportunity. If you can find a company that is having difficulties now but is likely to overcome those difficulties in the near future, its stock may very well be poised to skyrocket above current price levels. In that case, you will have found one of the best bargains around.

• Finding a true bargain gives you a double advantage—a greater potential for capital growth, and also a greater degree of safety. In other words, Templeton says, "If you buy an asset for one half or one fourth what you think it's worth, there is less risk of it going down than if you paid full value for it." The validity of this principle has been borne out time and time again in Templeton's investment experience, as his Templeton Growth Fund has turned in superior performances in down markets as well as in boom times.

• Right now common stocks are the best investment opportunity around, in Templeton's view. Below are the four reasons that led him to this decision.

Reason 1: Share prices are extremely cheap in relation to replacement values. There have been only three times in American history when share prices were as low as they have been recently, in relation to the *stated assets* of those corporations. In each of those three past periods, the low prices proved to be a temporary phenomenon: If an investor had significant holdings in common stocks during those three periods, he would have reaped a virtual bonanza in later years.

The "stated values" of a corporation refer to the "book values," or the values determined at the time the assets were acquired. When the effects of inflation on the various items of equipment, buildings and other assets of a company are taken into account, the asset values go much higher. So the corporation's worth in terms of the *replacement values* of its assets—or the amount of money it would take to replace those assets at current prices—must be set at a much higher figure. In fact, in August, 1982, stock prices in the United States were lower in relation to replacement values than they had ever been before in the history of the stock market.

Reason 2: Other nations' stock prices are relatively high in comparison with U.S. prices. Templeton says, "In the past few years we have gotten used to the concept of low stock prices in Canada and in the United States. But if you are studying investments worldwide, you will find that this psychology doesn't apply in many other places."

When he recently did a study of American and Canadian stocks in comparison with those of other countries, he discovered the following: "Canadian stocks were about eight times earnings, and American stocks were seven times earnings. But in Singapore stocks were sixteen times earnings; in Hong Kong, about eighteen times earnings; and in Japan, twenty times earnings."

So Templeton concludes: "That helps us to believe that might happen here. If it can happen in many other nations, then we may come to the time when America will have high price-to-earnings ratios again, and stock prices several times as high as now."

Reason 3: A high number of corporate takeovers suggests that stocks may now be good bargains. Corporations that understand the values of other corporations are often willing now to make offers to buy control of those companies. And when this happens they often pay more than 50 percent above the current stock-market price and can go to more than 100 percent over the market price.

Why are these corporations willing to pay so much to acquire other companies?

Templeton explains that "they do that because their superior knowledge of the industry causes them to think they are getting a bargain even at double what the stock market is appraising the stock."

Reason 4: More than at any previous time in history, corporations are buying up shares in their own companies. As officers and directors of many corporations look at the prices of their shares in the newspaper, "they can't understand why those shares are selling at such ridiculously low prices," Templeton says. So they use some of the cash the corporation has accumulated to buy up their own shares.

"That has been a growing trend, until there are now hundreds of companies that have bought or are buying their own shares," Templeton notes.

As a result of this practice, there are fewer shares outstanding, and so the earnings per share increase. That's a benefit for the remaining shareholders, because their stocks become more valuable. Also, the fact that a company is buying its own shares "proves that those people who know the company best believe that today's share prices are a real bargain," Templeton says.

Reason 5: Common stocks may soar in the next few years because there is a great deal of cash available for investment, and much of that cash may be used to buy shares of stock. "Share prices are not determined entirely by what they are worth," Templeton says. "They are also determined by who is going to buy them. Where is the money coming from to bid the price up? If there is no cash available, the share prices can stay very low. But there is more cash available now than I have ever seen in my life."

The sources of this cash include the following:

—Insurance companies, which traditionally buy a great deal of stock.

—Foreign investors, who are beginning to see that there are few places in the world where you can buy as much stock for so little money as you can in North America. The Japanese, Germans and Arabs are particularly active foreign buyers.

—Pension funds, which have the greatest accumulations of cash in the world. Today there is more than $600 billion in pension funds in the United States. And pension-fund experts are estimating that in about twelve years from now the pension funds of the United States alone may control more than $3 trillion!

Here is John Templeton's analysis of the pension-fund situation: "Suppose those pension funds were invested 50 percent in common stocks. At present, they hold about 55 percent in common stocks; and 55 percent has been about the average of pension-fund investments in common stocks throughout history.

"But to be conservative, as we should be, let's say that twelve years from now the pension funds might be 50 percent or more in common stocks. That means a one-and-a-half-trillion-dollar investment in common stocks by the pension funds!

"But how many common stocks are there? The *total* market value of all common stocks in the United States was about $1.25 trillion in August 1982. So we are saying that twelve years from now pension funds may have bought up more than 100 percent of all the common stocks currently outstanding in the United States!"

Templeton acknowledges that such a buying spree is "impossible—it's not going to happen. But what it illustrates is what *might* happen when pension funds try to put that much money into common stocks. The net effect of pension-fund acquisitions will bid up the prices of common stocks."

Templeton points to the case of General Motors, whose total pension funds are now worth about $17 billion. A couple of years ago, General Motors announced that they had 50 percent of their holdings in common stocks and that they were going to raise those stock holdings to 70 percent. This meant they would be putting additional billions of dollars into common stocks. If other managers of large pension funds begin to follow this same policy of buying more common stocks, a positive market psychology can begin to develop. The decision to buy stocks tends to "feed on itself," as Templeton puts it.

"There is a tendency for pension-fund managers to follow the leader," he explains. "Many of them may try to put his or her money into common stocks before others bid the prices up. And this can have a surprisingly strong influence on the price of all stocks."

Templeton thinks the same kind of market psychology that drove up the price of gold so dramatically in 1979 could at some future time influence stock prices. There are only 2.4 billion ounces of gold in the world; and so when people began to worry about inflation and saw gold as the best protection, the price of the metal spiraled up to more than $875 an ounce. A doubling of price occurred in just a few months' time.

"Speculators were rushing in, each one trying to buy up what little gold there was before somebody else bought it," Templeton said. "That same thing hasn't happened yet in common stocks. But I'm suggesting that sometime in the next six to eight years that type of psychology *might* develop in the ownership of common stocks. And common-stock prices might rise much higher than anyone now anticipates."

In fact, Templeton says, "My own guess is that there is a better than even chance that the Dow Jones Industrial Average can rise above three thousand sometime in the nineteen-eighties."

So, presently, John Templeton is almost fully invested in common stocks. Obviously, he feels right now the potential on the "upside" may be many times as great as the risk on the "downside."

But bargain-hunting, as important as it is, is only the first principle of that Templeton Touch which has made John Templeton one of the world's greatest investors. The next two principles—diversification, and broad social and political awareness—are just as important in their own way and deserve a separate chapter for a full explanation.

6

The Broad Business Principles

While bargain-hunting sets the basic tone for John Templeton's overall approach to investing, there are two other principles that are decisive in determining exactly where and how that hunting takes place. These two factors may be placed under the general heading "broad business principles" because they focus on sweeping trends and movements in the world's economics, rather than on personal skills and traits.

The first of these principles is diversification of investment holdings; and the second concerns the nature of the social and political systems where potential investments are based.

Principle Two: Diversification
"The only investors who shouldn't diversify are those who are right 100 percent of the time."

—John M. Templeton

This principle represents nothing new, of course. There is hardly anyone who doesn't believe in a well-diversified portfolio these days. The reason is simple: Diversified portfolios offer insurance against risk. If you have all your money in one stock and it declines, you lose heavily. But if you have only a *portion* of your money in one stock and it declines, you lose less.

On the other hand, if you're right about a certain stock and you have all your money invested in it, your return could be substantial. So that's why Templeton says, in the above quote, that if you're 100 percent sure you're right, don't diversify.

But his experience in investing has been that few people, including himself, are ever right more than two thirds of the time. That means that at least one third of the time even topflight investors are going to be wrong about a stock. So to protect yourself against those mistakes, it's absolutely essential to spread your risk.

As a guideline, Templeton recommends that every serious investor have at least ten stocks in his portfolio. To keep brokerage fees down, the stocks should be bought in 100-lot batches (100 shares of a given company at a time).

If you can't afford to achieve this degree of diversity on your own, then Templeton recommends that you buy shares in a mutual fund, which will automatically give you adequate diversification. The funds pool investors' money and then purchase hundreds of different stocks and bonds, thereby allowing smaller investors to buy a variety of shares that otherwise would be impossible for them.

Yet, even though Templeton agrees with other expert investors on the importance of diversification, he does have his own distinctive approach to the concept. He doesn't just search for securities in one industry or even in a variety of industries. Instead, he looks for his bargains worldwide. In other words, he diversifies among different companies within one industry; among different industries; and even among nations.

In this way, when a bear market hits the United States especially hard, Templeton's stocks generally don't suffer nearly as much as those of competitors who may be totally invested in American companies. His American stocks may not fare well, but his holdings in Japan, Canada and other nations can more than compensate.

Templeton explains his worldwide diversification method this way: "It's surprising how few investment firms and mutual funds take a worldwide viewpoint. But this is one of the contributing factors in our good performance, because it enables us to find more and better bargains.

"Equally important, the risk is reduced if your assets are diversified throughout many nations. Any one nation's economy fluctuates between bull markets and bear markets. At the same time, in other nations economic trends might be quite different. When the United States is experiencing a bad market, Japan may be having a boom.

"So if your assets are diversified throughout many nations, the impact of a United States bear market is lessened because the market doesn't fall in all the nations at the same time. The Templeton Growth Fund fared better than the competition in declining American markets than it did in rising markets because our investment portfolio included stocks in Canada, Japan, Australia and other places. That wide diversification has been one of the major keys to our success."

Principle Three: Broad Social and Political Awareness
"Avoid investing in those countries with a high level of socialism or government regulation of business. Business growth depends on a strong, free-enterprise system."
—John M. Templeton

Socialism, as Templeton defines it, means government ownership or extensive government regulation of business. One of the worst characteristics of socialism, Templeton feels, is that it empowers one small group of human beings to regulate the interests of the majority.

"That's a mistake," Templeton says. "You do have to have some minimum kind of government. But to the extent possible, governments should try to stop interfering with what people want to do."

In part, this attitude has its roots far back in John Templeton's childhood—those times when his mother was following her hands-off childrearing policy that allowed him to experiment with electricity, own a shotgun at age eight, and otherwise do pretty much as he wanted. His family life had given him a vivid, dramatic, firsthand experience of the benefits of human freedom; and the lessons he learned stayed with him for life.

Templeton's deep belief in the merits of free enterprise came into full flower as a professional investment counselor.

For example, when he had traveled around the world after graduating from Oxford, he had been especially struck by the poverty in India and Hong Kong. In Calcutta he saw people dying on the streets, and then their corpses were gathered up at night and placed on a pile of sticks called "ghats" and burned. The situation in Hong Kong was just as desperate.

When he returned years later to both these cities, he noticed a tremendous difference. In Calcutta there had been little or no improvement. In Hong Kong, however, there was a dramatic increase in prosperity.

"Hong Kong is now one of the most prosperous areas in the world," Templeton says. "And the major difference is the difference between free enterprise and socialism. The government of India regulates nearly everything, so there's very little progress; whereas in Hong Kong the government keeps its hands off. There are all kinds of enterprise flourishing. The standard of living in Hong Kong has multiplied more than tenfold in forty years, while the standard of living in Calcutta has improved hardly at all."

Templeton also cites Switzerland as an example of a land which has become "the wealthiest non-oil-producing nation in the world" because of its free-enterprise orientation. In contrast, he says, "nations that are far richer in terms of natural resources have remained poor because of social controls."

What are some of the specifics that the investor should consider, in light of Templeton's analysis of the advantages of free enterprise over socialism?

He believes that the problem that socialism poses for the investor can "hardly be overemphasized." Seventy years ago, he argues, an investor was not much concerned with political systems, but now the issue is much more pressing.

"If you're thinking of buying shares in a company that is likely to be the target of nationalization, you're not likely to get fair value if it is nationalized. Some nations actually confiscate a company and give no compensation. And even though most of them *say* they're going to pay, as a practical matter, getting fair compensation is a rarity."

Even without a complete government takeover, it's unwise to invest in companies that have been subjected to price controls. "Controls on hiring can be worked with, as can controls on product advertising and marketing. But rate regulation or price regulation are unacceptable practices. The main problem is that, for political reasons, rate and price regulation are usually so unfairly administered."

In the American political system he is also wary of investing in electric utilities which are subject to rate regulation. "There's no state that allows fair return on investment based on what it would cost to reproduce their assets," he explains. "They only allow utilities to earn a return on what they originally paid for their assets. Consequently, there is no protection against inflation."

Occasionally Templeton has invested in an electric utility company, but only when the price of the stock was so low that, despite inflation, the investment was a true bargain.

The guiding principle that John Templeton has in mind as he searches the world for bargains is that "great prosperity occurs only when people are free. If we regulate people excessively, we slow down and perhaps prevent—or, conceivably, even reverse—the trend toward prosperity.

As an illustration of this, Templeton was one of the first foreigners to invest in Japan after World War II. When he began investing there, you were permitted to buy Japanese stocks, but if you sold them you had to leave the money in Japan. As a result, very few foreigners were buying Japanese stocks.

But Japanese stocks were real bargains because the nation had just been defeated in the war, and most investors weren't even thinking of Japan as a potential industrial power. Templeton knew better. He had studied the Japanese people and their government very closely, and he liked what he saw:

"The Japanese people are wonderfully hard workers," he notes. "The savings rate of the people in Japan was then and still is twenty-five cents out of every dollar they earn, whereas in America in the early nineteen-eighties, the savings rate is down to five cents out of each dollar. The Japanese are very thrifty, and their thrift enables them to spend more money for plant improvements and new methods. Their work attitudes, even today, are the way attitudes were in the United States sixty years ago. The Japanese people are really happy about their employers, and they consider it a privilege to work for a fine company. Some work on Saturdays. And they admire businessmen. All these things have led to prosperity for Japanese corporations and the Japanese public.

And these considerations have entered into my estimate of what I'm willing to pay for shares of Japanese stock."

So back in the early nineteen-fifties, Templeton got in touch with a Japanese broker who could speak English. He gathered what information he could about various Japanese stocks, and then he invested a considerable part of his savings in them. Within a few years the restriction on removing capital from Japan was changed, so that foreigners were free to take their capital gains out of Japan.

At that point Templeton began to invest not only his own money, but also that of his clients, in Japanese companies. There were so many bargains that, before long, almost 50 percent of the total assets of his Templeton Growth Fund were in Japanese companies. And these heavy holdings in Japanese stocks were one of the reasons the Templeton Growth Fund has turned in such a superior performance during the past three decades.

The importance of studying the laws and politics of a country are a key factor in Templeton's Japanese success story. Specifically, he studied the peculiarities of the Japanese business scene and found that the Japanese had an unusual way of reporting their earnings. In the United States the term "earnings" means the consolidated earnings of the *entire* company. But in Japan the term means the earnings of the *parent* company. For example, suppose a parent company owns several subsidiaries. One of those subsidiaries earns $1 million and passes on only $10 to the parent company. Then suppose that $9.00 out of that $10 is used for parent-company expenses. The unwary investor may see only $1 as parent-company earnings from that subsidiary operation—when the *actual* earnings of the subsidiary were $1 million.

So Templeton saw that the important earnings figures to look at in Japanese companies are the *consolidated* earnings of all of a parent company's subsidiaries, not just the earnings of the parent company. As a result, he looked around Japan for the company which had the largest consolidated earnings as compared with the earnings of its parent company. That company turned out to be Hitachi Ltd., the electronics manufacturer. Hitachi had consolidated earnings which were roughly two and a half times the parent-company earnings.

Templeton got the jump on even the Japanese by understanding the significance of this peculiarity of Japanese accounting. The Japanese buyers of Hitachi and other stocks were looking only at the parent-company earnings, which were relatively low, and not the consolidated earnings, which were much higher. In the case of Hitachi, the assumption was that the stock was selling for about sixteen times earnings. But Templeton, who was focusing on the larger, consolidated earnings, saw that the stock was selling at only six times earnings.

Templeton believed that when the Japanese perceived that the true Hitachi earnings were much higher than they had assumed, they would bid the stock up to a higher level.

"The likelihood that Japanese investors would bid Hitachi up to two and a half times the price they had previously put on it made it a bargain," Templeton said. "Attitudes of investors in Japan are slow to change, and for many years they rarely thought about consolidated earnings. Then the Japanese Government began to require companies to report consolidated earnings, and one Japanese investor after another started looking at the consolidated earnings."

Templeton acted on what he already knew about the consolidated earnings and purchased the bargain-priced Hitachi market before many of the Japanese did. "It's still just beginning to dawn on some investors," Templeton says. "So we're still holding the stock. If and when the price moves up into line with other Japanese stocks, then it will no longer be a bargain, and we'll buy something else."

What does John Templeton think may be the Japan of the future for investors? Perhaps it will be South Korea. He hasn't yet invested any of his clients' capital there, because South Korea has some restrictions on removal of funds, as Japan once had. An individual can invest money, but profits must be left in South Korea.

Still, he says, "I believe, in the long run, the South Korean laws restricting removal of capital will be changed." And if they are, there may well be another Hitachi for his clients.

So an important part of John Templeton's search for investment bargains involves looking for political and social contexts where free enterprise is thriving. And when he finds an environment that's favorable to the entrepreneurial spirit, he studies the political and social situations there in even greater detail to learn how he can shape their characteristics to his advantage.

Even though there are many things about each nation that are unique, one problem is common to most contemporary governments: inflation.

"One fundamental thing that is built into every system of politics and into human nature is that each of us wants more," Templeton says. "And because we want more, we force prices up. Eighty-five percent of the total cost of goods, including outlays for facilities, production and distribution, is labor. And if people want higher wages and higher salaries, the net result is to force up the cost of production."

He believes that this upward pressure has a direct effect on inflation and will lead to periods when the rate of inflation will be as high as 20 percent a year in the United States, even without a war or marked increase of government control.

"Outside the United States, inflation is likely to be higher because there are fewer economic and political controls. Currently, we see an annual 100 percent inflation rate in Argentina, Brazil, Israel and several other places. It's not impossible that this sort of thing could happen in the United States also."

Templeton doesn't expect that a catastrophe will drive up inflation rates in the United States to those extremely high levels. Instead, he thinks the inflation rate in the United States will range between 3 percent and 20 percent for the next couple of decades. But inflation as high as 20 percent is still of great concern. How can an investor protect himself? Templeton suggests these guidelines:

• You should invest in nations which have a record of relatively low inflation rates.

• Divest yourself of cash or of anything denominated in cash, such as bonds, mortgages and life insurance.

• Maximize protection by investing in equities—including real estate and stocks.

As a cautionary note concerning real estate, there have been cases, such as in France, where, with rapid inflation, the government has placed a strict set of controls on rents. In such a situation, the ownership of an apartment or rental house proved to be worthless because it cost more to operate than the owner could recover in rents. But in most instances of inflation throughout history, the ownership of real estate was the biggest single way to protect yourself, Templeton says.

In recent years the stock market in America hasn't been a particularly good hedge against inflation, but experts like Templeton, who have known where to look for bargains, have beaten the inflation rate handily. All that's necessary is to examine the record of the Templeton Growth Fund over the past two or three decades, as you saw at the beginning of Chapter 5, to understand what is possible in the stock market.

• You should give serious consideration to stocks of companies that are heavily in debt. "Fifty years ago, before inflation became important, most security analysts preferred to buy the stock of a company that was debt-free. But now, because inflation has become so important, many investors, including ourselves, are seriously looking at stocks of companies that have heavy debt."

The two principles of diversification and of broad social and political awareness have been essential elements in John Templeton's great success as an investor. His commitment to these principles, and especially to the idea of a worldwide quest for bargains, are among the most distinctive features of his investment style. But perhaps even more important—if not quite so high-profile and public—are those personal qualities and characteristics that have made John Templeton the great success he is.

7

The Personal Side of the Templeton Touch

The third group of principles that have enabled John Marks Templeton to reach the pinnacle among the world's investors are very personal. They are a composite of beliefs and character traits that distinguish John Templeton, the man, from most other individuals. Yet, despite the fact that these characteristics are an integral part of Templeton's unique personality, they can all be developed and cultivated to some degree by anyone—provided the desire, ambition and self-discipline are there.

Here, then, are the next seven basic principles, which make up the personal side of the Templeton Touch:

Principle Four: Flexibility

"If you want to produce the best results in twenty or thirty years, you have to be flexible. A flexible viewpoint is a matter of avoiding a peculiar trait of human nature, which is to buy the things that you wish you had bought in the past, or to continue to buy the things that did well for you in the past."

—John M. Templeton

Most investors, John Templeton says, are "inflexible" in their approach to certain types of investments, and as a result, their performance over the long haul is not what it should be. By "inflexible" he means that these investors tend to gravitate consistently toward one type of investment or another—such as small companies, Japanese companies, or some other definite group. When that particular group is doing well, then those investors do well. But when that group is doing poorly, those investors don't have the necessary flexibility to shift to another, more profitable group of stocks.

The reason for this lack of flexibility, Templeton explains, is that "almost everyone who undertakes to select investments is either a specialist or unconsciously a specialist. For example, you will have an investor who looks only at growth stocks; or another who looks only at Japanese stocks.

"And if they do that, then sometimes, for a year or several years, they will have a wonderful record because those stocks are becoming popular. To use a relatively recent example, a couple of years ago those mutual funds that had the best record were the funds in the smaller companies. That particular year that area of specialization was just right, and those funds turned in performances that looked wonderful."

And how can an investor ensure that he or she will remain as flexible as possible?

To achieve that goal, Templeton says you must "always try to examine seriously what area has done well for you for several years. Then you say, 'Well, now, maybe that's not the place for us to be in the future.' Suppose you've got a group of stocks—say, oil and gas stocks—that have contributed to your good performance for two or three years in a row. If that's the case, then you should try hard to look around and ask, 'Well, what is it *today* that is depressed in price?' Those things that helped you so much in the last two or three years can't be the bargains they were when you first bought them. So instead of staying in those things that have treated you well in the past, you should be looking for those things that performed *worst* in the past—and consider buying those now."

It's not that he thinks that the worst performers in the past will necessarily be among the best performers today—*because* they were so bad. Rather, those "dogs" of years gone by may be worth buying today because they have become undervalued, as most investors have avoided buying them. Templeton's approach is to search for those investments that have performed badly for reasons that are temporary rather than permanent. The net effect is that he is always trying to shift into some investment area where today's bargains are—rather than continually focusing on the bargains of the past. He explains the point this way:

"If you go to parties and talk to people about investments, some will say, 'Oh, I wish I had loaded up with those oil and gas stocks!' And so they're loading up with them now. Or they say, 'Oh, I wish I had been in common stocks instead of bonds,' and so they're buying common stocks. Or at a time when the stock market has been bad for years and is probably poised for a major recovery, they say, 'Oh, I wish I didn't have any common stocks. I wish I had all my money in some good bonds.' So they start loading up with bonds—at the precise time when they should be buying stocks."

Templeton believes there is something basic in human nature which causes almost everyone to load up with those investments they wish they had owned five years ago. "But that's just the wrong thing to do!" he observes. "What they should be doing is searching around and asking, 'Where is some property that has been unpopular in the past and is now depressed in price?'"

In choosing stocks for a flexible program, there are three things to keep in mind:

• You won't be right all the time. "When we shift from one stock to another, we're not right all the time," Templeton concedes. "We may shift out of growth stocks into high-quality stocks, but that may be a wrong decision. In order to be flexible in investment management and preserve your freedom to shift around, you can't expect that every decision you make is going to be right. But the net result over twenty or thirty years is going to be better than if you didn't try to be flexible."

• An investor has to be consistent and self-disciplined. When deciding to shift into an unpopular or depressed stock, there will probably be feelings of uncertainty and one may even get a little "rattled" or nervous. Being the only one who has invested in a particular stock or group of stocks provokes worry. Don't be a maverick just for the sake of being contrary. On the other hand, if you've studied the company or industry thoroughly and there's no reason to change your opinion about the outlook for your investment, then stick to your guns! One of the things that has made John Templeton so successful as an investor is that he has the personal discipline and self-confidence to stay with an investment decision until the price rises or until the facts prove him wrong.

• To achieve the best results from a flexible investment program, stocks or other property may have to be held for a long, long time. "The great majority of people are looking at the short range—what's going to have higher earnings next month or next year," Templeton says. "But we focus on what a company could earn two years or five years from now." And that brings us to the next major personal trait of a great investor—patience.

Principle Five: Patience
"One of the reasons our performance is said to be the best investment record in the world on a twenty- to twenty-five-year basis is that we've always tried to look ahead—and the long-range view requires patience."

—John M. Templeton

Because most people are looking only at the short-term performance of stocks, those investments are not the bargains. "Often, when we get into something that we are sure is a bargain, it remains a bargain for years," Templeton says. "In other words, it doesn't move up in price. This type of investment takes a lot of patience, but usually it pays off."

The reason it pays off, he says, is that eventually other people come along who have a short-range viewpoint. They see that the same stocks Templeton has held for a relatively long time now have the potential to increase in the near future. Templeton may have projected that a certain company was going to have very high earnings five years in the future. Then, as that five-year goal gets closer, people with a short-range viewpoint begin to see the high earnings potential, and they start to bid the stock up in price.

"So I guess the basic principle is this: If you apply the same methods of selection that other people are applying, you'll get the same things they're buying and you'll have the same record they have. But we try to have a longer-range viewpoint—and the patience that goes along with it. So we try to buy those things that others have not yet thought about. Then we *wait* until the short-term prospects become good and other people start coming in and buying the stock and pushing the price up."

But just because Templeton is willing to exercise considerable patience in waiting for a bargain to become generally recognized doesn't mean he's uninterested in cutting down the waiting time.

"In a few cases we've found that we can reduce the holding time for certain bargain stocks," he notes. "When we are searching through hundreds of stocks, we'll find on a given day that there are, say, twelve stocks which are hard to choose among. They appear to be equally good bargains.

"But then we look at their price patterns: If two out of those twelve have already started to move up, then we buy those, because they're just as good bargains as those that aren't moving. So we may not have to hold them for long before they rise in price and provide a good profit."

But even with techniques such as this to reduce his holding period for stocks, Templeton still finds that his average holding period is about six years at the present time. Still, he's quick to point out that maintaining a certain average holding period for his stocks is not part of any "system" that he's developed as an investor. On the contrary, he vehemently denies that he has any system at all: He's just a bargain-hunter who has certain procedures that help him search for the best buy.

"Benjamin Graham did feel that if he bought a stock, thinking it was the best bargain, and in two or three years it hadn't proved to be a good bargain, then he should change," Templeton says, referring to the great investment guru who was once his teacher. "Too much changing is too expensive. And so at present I'm holding things longer than four or five years. But the time period isn't really the thing that guides me in making my decision. If you find something that's an excellent bargain, in order to buy it you have to sell something else. And so I look over my list to see which stock that I own is the least good bargain—and I sell that.

"But in this process I haven't asked myself whether I've owned the stock one week or twenty years. It makes no difference! It's only when I look at the history of what I did that I find I have an average holding period of about six years."

So there are many facets to the quality of patience which has played such an important role in John Templeton's rise to preeminence in the investing field. But along with this patience must go a special kind of hard work; and that brings us to the next key investment principle in the Templeton Touch.

Principle Six: Extensive Analytical Research
of Each Investment Opportunity

"One of the best ways to evaluate an industry is to ask various company presidents which stock they would invest in, other than their own."

—John M. Templeton

The backbone of John Templeton's tremendous success as an investor is the hours of study and thought that he devotes to his work. Although it may seem trite to say that he has made it to the top because he works hard, there is a great deal of truth in that statement. But it would be even more accurate to say that his hard work and thorough research put him in a position to exercise his considerable powers of discernment and good judgment to their fullest.

It's also important to note here that John Templeton doesn't just delegate the research tasks to those who work for him. To be sure, he does have a number of assistants, officers and other employees in his companies who contribute a great deal to the formulation of the portfolios that have made the Templeton approach to investing the most successful in the world.

But in the last analysis, the buck stops with John Templeton on all decisions as to which stocks should be bought and which should be sold. He gives the final "yes" or "no." And that means he must do a prodigious amount of personal research so that he can make an informed decision about what to do with each company that comes up for his consideration.

Here are several of the key research techniques that have enabled Templeton to succeed as an investor:

• *Quantitative analysis.* When Templeton first started out as an investment counselor, there were hundreds of security analysts he had to compete with, and they mostly relied on a method of stock evaluation called "qualitative analysis." As they began to study a company, they would ask things like: Is this a growth industry? Is this company financially strong? Is it well managed? Does it face strong competition? Or if they researched a particular company like General Electric, they might conclude: "General Electric has good earning power, a good profit margin, and good management."

This approach, then, described a company in terms of its *qualities*. But the problem with this method was that there was no way to combine these qualitative concepts and then compare them with other companies. Templeton saw the drawbacks of this technique, and so he began to stress the numerical distinctions between different aspects of a given company's performance. He was a pioneer in the science of "quantitative analysis."

"When I began, no other security analyst I knew was using quantitative analysis," he recalls. "This method had a lot to do with the fact that we were able to produce such a good performance record for our mutual funds. Quantitative analysis is in widespread use today: In a world of about twenty thousand professional security analysts, I think more than 10 percent now use this approach. But we were one of the first."

How exactly does quantitative analysis work?

Whereas investors using qualitative analysis rely on general descriptions of a company's performance, those employing quantitative analysis stress arithmetic. Using the General Electric example above, then, you would say: "General Electric earns 16.7 percent on invested capital. It's growing at an average yearly rate of 13.0 percent. And it's getting a 2 percent higher share of the market than its competitors."

"With quantitative analysis, the knowledge of a company is expressed not in words but in numbers," Templeton says. "By putting the information into arithmetic, you have a lot of advantages: For example, you can compare industries, such as the electrical and oil industries, to see which is a better bargain. If you couldn't put this information into figures, there would be no solid basis for comparison."

In pursuing this technique of quantitative analysis, Templeton believes that "one of the first things you should look at is the earning power through the common practice of reviewing the price-earnings record. You should examine how cheap a stock is. You're not interested so much in this year's earnings or past earnings, as in possible earnings five to ten years in the future."

After placing a numerical value on the estimated future earnings of a company, then review the given company's management. For example, instead of saying, "This management is strong," or "This management is weak," be more specific: You might determine that a certain management is increasing its total share of the market by ½ percent a year in relation to its competitors. Or the management is getting an average return on its invested capital that is 9 percent a year greater than its competitors can achieve. You might also find that the management is getting 1 percent a year higher profit margin on its sales; and the company's annual growth is 4 percent greater than the growth of its competitors.

"In this way, because you've got the arithmetic, you've got quantities," Templeton explains. "You measure the management by quantities rather than by qualities. So arithmetic does two things for you: It enables you to take the different aspects of a corporation and combine them in arithmetic terms in order to arrive at a valuation estimate for that corporation. And secondly, stressing numbers enables you to compare different types of corporations by what they score in terms of their arithmetic total."

Quantitative analysis has been perhaps the single most important selling point for Templeton's approach to stock selection— aside from the fact that he has had such a brilliant track record for more than two decades. "I've made a career of quantitative analysis," he said. "We built our list of clients by showing them the advantages of quantitative analysis and explaining it to them. We showed them what we were doing that was different from other investment counselors who were using qualitative analysis. Our quantitative analysis turned out to be a good way to attract clients, and it was also a good way to produce a superior record."

But obviously, quantitative analysis requires a great deal of study and work, and that brings us to the next key research technique.

• *Private study.* Templeton says that evaluating various stocks, including the application of quantitative analysis, is not too complicated for the average investor to attempt. But he adds, "I would offer a word of caution. Selecting investments is a competitive experience. You should ask yourself before you undertake it: Are you going to work at it enough so that you'll become better than your average competitor? If not, you'll gradually lose out. On the other hand, if you are better than your average competitor, you will gradually win. So if you're a part-time investor of if you're not sure of your abilities, you're better off hiring an expert to do it for you."

And by "expert" he means a mutual fund, a professional investment counselor or a trust company.

If you decide you're going to devote enough time to studying various stocks and you honestly believe you have the potential to be wiser than the average person who is buying and selling stocks, then "you can do it," Templeton says. "And you should do it by quantitative methods."

Specifically, he spends his typical working week this way: He works about sixty hours a week. Roughly half of that time is devoted to his nonprofit religious activities, including the Templeton Foundation Program of Prizes for Progress in Religion, and about half is devoted to investment management.

During the hours he spends in reading and studying various companies, he concentrates on financial services and other sources. "We subscribe to more than a hundred different financial publications and services," he notes. These include the Value Line investment service, the *Wall Street Journal,* and a variety of studies put out by security analysts from the one hundred brokerage firms that the Templeton companies do business with.

Here are a few tips he has to offer about some of the most important written sources he relies upon:

—The *Wall Street Journal* gives him much of the key general political and business news he needs to make investment decisions. "If you find from the *Wall Street Journal* that the price of world sugar has gone down from 20 cents a pound to 6 cents a pound, that could change your evaluation of a dozen different companies. So the *Wall Street Journal* is a very useful secondary source of information. But Templeton focuses on the second and third columns from the left on the front page of the *Journal* for much of his information, because "these sections contain excellent summaries of major news developments." He tends to scan the rest of the paper, as well as any other papers he reads.

"Scanning is an absolutely essential skill for an investor today," he says, "because of the huge volume of information available. I find there are usually only four or five stories in any publication that are worth my serious attention. Scanning helps me find those stories as quickly as possible and not get bogged down in articles of less importance."

—The Value Line service is one of his favorites "because Value

Line specializes in putting the most important facts about a corporation on one page. Over the forty years they've been working on it, they've learned how to pack into that page the largest amount of relevant figures and facts. Also, they arrange the information in a way that makes it easy to compare one corporation with another. For example, they adjust to allow for stock splits and other things that might make it hard to compare different time periods or different companies. So on one page in Value Line I can get as much information in ten minutes as I could get in talking with the president of that company for many hours."

—"But the most valuable of all the secondary sources are our contacts with other security analysts," Templeton says.

Analysts in various brokerage firms publish, on average, about thirty public analyses of various corporations in one year. "So in a year's time we may look at as many as three thousand security analysis studies, and from those we pick out about three hundred that deserve further study. From those three hundred we would normally invest in about a hundred and fifty different companies in about twelve different nations."

Of course, Templeton has ready access to many free publications by a variety of security analysts because he does a considerable amount of business with them. But what about the average investor who doesn't have the advantage of investing about $2 billion of other people's money? How can he or she gain access to this information?

Templeton suggests the public library for some of the many investment advisory services that are published in the United States. In addition, if you throw all your business to one stockbroker, that broker should be happy to allow you to use his Value Line service, Standard and Poor's Stock Reports, the reports by his firm's security analysts, and various other resources. If he isn't willing to help you do your own research, it would be a good idea to find a broker who will give you more assistance, Templeton advises.

So John Templeton puts emphasis on studying and reading secondary sources and then putting the information in those sources to work through quantitative analysis. But there is one other important aspect of his research—the face-to-face encounter with top corporate management.

• *Interviews with Top Executives.* When Templeton first started out as an investment counselor he spent a vast amount of time talking to executives of various companies in personal interviews. More recently, he has found that "what comes in from secondary sources is far more valuable than what comes directly." But he and his staff still make use of the personal interview, and after more than forty years of experience he has become quite an expert.

"Usually the significant things to ask top executives relate to the future," he says. "You can get all the past facts from their published records. But you're also interested in their long-range plans, and this information will be more current and complete if you spend some time talking to them."

But the interview question that Templeton has found most valuable is the final one he puts to a corporate officer: "If you were going to buy shares, and you couldn't buy shares in your own company, which one of your competitors, suppliers or customers would you buy shares in—and why?"

He has found that this question "leads to marvelous information. The people who know the industry best can put their finger quickly on which company is going to forge ahead and why, or which is going to lag behind and why. And they will do it much more quickly than they will for their own company. Almost every executive is optimistic about his own company, and he may talk for hours about it. But if you ask him about a competitor, in thirty seconds he'll give you the lowdown on that company."

Some might feel that a businessman's appraisal of a competitor is likely to be biased, or even less than honest in order to throw off a potential investor like Templeton. But he has discovered otherwise.

"The standard of ethics among top businessmen is the highest in any field I know of," he says. "I work a lot with Christian ministers, and with lawyers and accountants and professionals of all types. But after years of thinking about it, I don't believe there is any area where ethics are as high as they are with the top people in big corporations."

So he trusts what they tell him. And over the years his trust in them and his reliance on their information has paid off in outstanding investments.

The principle of "extensive, analytical research" demands a

great deal of time and energy from John Templeton. In contrast, there are four other principles of topflight investing that play a lesser role; but each, in its own way, has been instrumental in Templeton's success.

Principle Seven: An Extensive Friendship Network

"If I want to know something about a particular industry, I just call a friend who has spent his life in that industry."

—John M. Templeton

Throughout his life John Templeton has stayed in touch with a wide variety of personal and business acquaintances, and they have helped keep him informed about investment opportunities. They are, in every sense of the word, "good contacts," but he prefers to call them "friends."

That word is probably most appropriate because he *likes* people; he's naturally a gregarious person. But even though he may not establish many of his personal relationships primarily for business purposes, there is no doubt that they have come in quite handy when he's trying to make an investment decision.

"These hundreds of friends with whom I have a first-name relationship in almost every industry and in a variety of nations, are a wonderful help in selecting investments. If I want to know something about the banking industry in England, for example, I'll pick up the telephone and talk to a friend who has spent his life in that industry. The information sources are marvelous."

Many of Templeton's business friendships have arisen as a result of particular jobs or investment research he has worked on. But there have also been more formal, structured vehicles he has used—notably the Young Presidents Organization and the Chief Executives Organization.

He became one of the charter members of the Young Presidents Organization after Ray Hickock, the twenty-five-year-old president of the Hickock Belt Company, sponsored a luncheon for fifty potential members at the Waldorf-Astoria in New York City back in 1950. Hickock's father had died and left him in charge of the belt and leather company at an exceptionally young age. But young Hickock felt a need to talk with other young executives about the techniques and basic questions of management. So he asked his public relations agent, Philip Schuyler, to get in touch with some other young chief executives. And John Templeton was one of those invited to the luncheon.

As a result of this meeting, seventeen of the fifty who attended Hickock's luncheon decided they would like to meet on a regular basis in the future—and the Young Presidents Organization began. At first the requirements for membership were that the person become president of a corporation before he reached age forty. Also, his company had to have a sales volume of $3 million a year or have assets of at least $50 million. These sales-assets criteria changed over the years, but the age requirement remained the same.

Another qualification for membership in this group was that you had to drop out when you reached age forty-nine. But when Templeton and some of his colleagues reached that age they decided they wanted to continue their friendships. So they formed an alumni organization for the Young Presidents Organization which they called the Chief Executives Organization. All were graduates of Y.P.O. and there was no upper age limit. Templeton served as president of that organization at one time.

These two groups are formal expressions of an approach to people that has become a way of life for John Templeton. When a person is talking with him, the topics of conversation may drift from personal subjects to religious concepts to business. And in most cases those conversations will be easygoing, pleasant and to the point. But Templeton is likely to carry away something important that he can use in one of his business or philanthropic projects. His personal relationships, as natural and friendly as they are, are likely to be conducted as efficiently and productively as anything else he does.

Principle Eight: Thought Control
"When St. Paul recites the fruits of the Spirit, one of those nine fruits is self-control. In my opinion, each human being should give much more attention to what is going on in his own mind. A person is what he thinks, and if you want to be a better person, you have to control what you're thinking."
—John M. Templeton

John Templeton frequently mentions and advocates what he calls "thought control." But his concept of controlling your thoughts has nothing to do with popular notions associated with religious cults or political brainwashing. What he's talking about is a voluntary internal discipline which involves "taking control of your own mind and using it for purposes that you believe are worthwhile and admirable."

Templeton's prodigious powers of concentration, perseverance and hard work can be traced in large part to his development of personal techniques of thought control. And this is a form of self-discipline that he believes is within the reach of anyone—if a person will only resolve to develop this special personal power.

"Everyone has to work at it," Templeton says. "And the more you work at it, the easier it gets. A person will say to you, 'I can't control my thoughts! They always wander away!' But that's because they haven't been trying. If you sit down at the piano and say, 'I can't play,' well, you *can't* play because you haven't worked at it. But if you work at playing the piano, you'll gradually find it easier and easier. The same is true with thought control."

Templeton acknowledges that there are some people, especially those involved in Eastern religions, who are quite successful at thought-restricting meditation. "But making your mind blank is extremely difficult, and to restate an old maxim, 'An idle mind really *is* the devil's workshop.'"

In contrast, the thought-control technique he advocates is what he calls the "crowding-out method." He explains his approach this way: "If you fill up the entire capacity of your mind with thoughts that you think are good and productive, you won't have room for the others. The ones you try to crowd out are feelings of envy, hatred, covetousness, self-centeredness, criticism, revenge—and also any time-wasting thoughts that are unproductive for your ultimate goals in life."

In practical terms, he employs the crowding-out thought-control method by spending his free time reading and studying publications that relate to his career and his philanthropic interests. As has been mentioned, he always carries papers and articles around with him to read when he's traveling or waiting for an appointment. Also, to keep a relaxed frame of mind and avoid the anxiety and pressures that can accompany chronic lateness, he puts a heavy stress on punctuality: He sets his watch ten to fifteen minutes ahead of time, and always tries to arrive at appointments at least ten minutes early. Then, if he has to wait for the appointment to begin, he pulls out his papers and uses the time to good advantage. Because he almost always carries reading material, he never gets annoyed if the other person is running late. "When I arrive at the appointment, I just start right to work on matters I've been anxious to get to. Whether the others are late or not doesn't matter much."

But as active and hardworking as Templeton is, he does periodically find he has to sit back in a state of relative repose and ponder the meaning of the voluminous reading he does. "But it's *directed* thinking. It shouldn't be thinking that is uncontrolled."

And he has a deep aversion to pastimes that most people regard as a normal part of their lives—television and movies. In fact, he rarely even reads novels. "I don't have time," he says. "There are too many more important things that make demands on my life."

So John Templeton keeps a close watch on everything that passes before his eyes or drifts into range of his hearing. As a result, he is able to focus a maximum amount of his energies on those things he feels are of supreme importance—his investments and his religious commitments. And his comprehensive method of thought control has caused the tone of his entire life to become thoroughly positive.

Principle Nine: Positive Thinking
"I expect the production of the world to double in the next eighteen years."

—John M. Templeton

Many words might be used to describe John Marks Templeton: "calm," "even-tempered," "gentle," "efficient," "kind," "incredibly hardworking," "highly disciplined," "reserved." But perhaps the term that comes closest to the essence of his personality is "positive thinking."

Templeton is quick to identify himself as a positive thinker too: "Yes, I would definitely describe myself that way. I'm so grateful and thankful for the millions of blessings that God gives us, for having been born in this particular time, that I can't see how anybody could be anything except joyous all day long. In addition to that, I do believe that positive thinking is a great help—not only in spiritual growth and human relations, but a help in financial matters and every other activity in life."

He has found that one of the major characteristics of the members of the Young Presidents Organization he has known is optimism. "It's very difficult to build a corporation if you're a pessimist. You almost have to be an optimist to build any substantial organization, whether it's a business or a church or a charity. To be successful, you have to *expect* success."

Now, such attitudes may seem like something out of *Pollyanna* —or just too good to be true. But this is a dimension of Templeton's thought-control technique that he has cultivated over a life time. And it's given him a "can do" attitude in everything he attempts, including his work as an investor.

It's important to understand, however, that his positive outlook doesn't arise from a life that has only seen success. Despite his obvious achievements, he cautions: "At one time I counted up more than a dozen business corporations or ventures which I started that were never successful."

To some people such failures are regarded as defeat, whereas to others they become challenges and opportunities to learn. John Templeton falls into this latter category. Long before Norman Vincent Peale became popular, he says, he was influenced by the philosophy of that popular song of the nineteen-forties about accentuating the positive and eliminating the negative.

Of course, it is possible to argue that John Templeton is *so* positive that he's sometimes incapable of seeing the negative side of a situation. For example, when he says that he expects world production to double in the next eighteen years, or that he thinks chances are even that the Dow Jones Industrial Average will hit three thousand by 1988,* one may wonder if any other viewpoint is possible for him. Or is he so positive by nature that something deep inside makes it necessary for him to hold such a rosy view of the future?

Certainly, his positive beliefs are extremely deep-rooted: They can be traced all the way back to the religious influences of his childhood, as we'll see in the next chapter. They are an inextrica-

* This estimate was made on the "Wall Street Week" television program on June 18, 1982, when the Dow Jones was 788.

ble part of his nature and must influence his long-range views on the economy—just as the views of those "doomsayers" who are always seeing a currency crisis or economic collapse around the corner must be shaped by a much darker personal outlook on the future.

So it's helpful to keep John Templeton's underlying positive thinking in mind when evaluating his outlook on the longer-range prospects for the American and world economies. But it's also essential not to allow an emphasis on his positive thinking to overshadow the realism of his in-depth market research and the hardheaded way he evaluates one corporation against another. He's certainly no Pollyanna when it comes to dumping a loser in favor of a stock he considers a bargain.

On balance, Templeton's positive approach to life and business is a refreshing breeze in the midst of an overabundance of gloomy forecasts by naysaying pundits. Listen to a few of his upbeat observations on life:

• "If a stranger walks into the room, do you notice that he has a withered hand, or do you notice the smile on his face? You can plant in your mind a wonderful concept and a good relationship with that stranger if you look for what's good in him, not for what worries you about him."

• "You can find what you look for in a situation. I'm a great believer in this old story: A stranger came to the gates of a city and said, 'What kind of people live here?' The gatekeeper said, 'What kind of people live in the place where *you* came from?' The stranger said, 'Oh, they were knaves and fools and thugs.' The gatekeeper said, '*You* will find the same kind of people here.'

"Another stranger came to the gate and asked the same question, and the gatekeeper replied in the same way: 'What kind of people live in the place where *you* came from?' The second stranger said, 'The people in the city where I come from are loving and generous.' And the gatekeeper said, '*You* will find the same kind of people here.'

"That's what our lives are all about. And that's thought control. If you're looking for the good in every person, you'll ask, 'Where can I see Christ shining through in this man's personality or this woman's life?' And you'll find Him in almost everybody."

• "I've always liked that motto of the Christophers, which says,

'It's better to light one candle than to curse the darkness.' I believe that's part of the way God has structured His universe. Those people who are pursuing the positive get results, whereas those who are cursing the evil usually don't get very far."

• "As soon as you open your mind in the morning, think of five things that you're deeply grateful for. That will set the pattern for your day. You can't very well feel self-pity, you can't feel loneliness, you can't feel that you are discriminated against, if your mind is filled with thanksgiving."

• "We should be overwhelmingly grateful to have been born in this century. The slow progress of prehistoric ages is over, and centuries of human enterprise are now miraculously bursting into flower. The evolution of human knowledge is accelerating, and we are reaping the fruits of generations of scientific thought: More than half of the scientists who ever lived are alive today. More than half of the discoveries in the natural sciences have been made in this century. More than half of the goods produced since the earth was born have been produced in the twentieth century. Over half the books ever written were written in the last half century. More new books are published each month than were written in the entire historical period before the birth of Columbus." (From *The Humble Approach* by John M. Templeton.)

In many ways, then, John Templeton's entire personal and business life seems directed toward thoughts and actions which build up rather than tear down. In a sense, he consistently attempts to realize in practical, everyday terms the words of St. Paul in Philippians 4:8: "Finally, brethren, whatsoever things are true, whatsoever things are honest, whatsoever things are just, whatsoever things are pure, whatsoever things are lovely, whatsoever things are of good report; if there be any virtue, and if there be any praise, think on these things."

Perhaps more than any other passage of Scripture, these words have in practice become the slogan for both his private and professional life.

Principle Ten: Simplicity
"When looking for a good stock, just remain 'simple-minded.'"

—John M. Templeton

John Templeton is anything but "simpleminded," in the sense of being uninformed or foolish. But after he has plumbed the depths of information about a given industry or company, he always tries to distill the essence of that industry or company as an investment opportunity. He tries to state the strengths and weaknesses of a prospective purchase as clearly and simply as possible. And the result is that in most cases his investment decisions become relatively easy to make.

"Don't get too complicated," Templeton warns. "Don't get into complex mathematical formulas, and don't try to dig too deeply into the details of every corporation. Just remain 'simpleminded' and look for the basic principles."

Those simple principles of Templeton's include:

• "If you buy what other people are buying, you're going to have the same performance as other people. You haven't got a chance of having a better performance unless you buy different things than other people buy. It's surprising that not everybody knows this right away, but obviously they don't."

• "Buy the best bargains."

• "If you're going to buy the best bargains, you have to buy the things that other people are selling."

• "If you're going to buy the best bargains, look in more than one industry, and look in more than one nation."

• "There is an old saying that when any company or industry gets on the front pages of the newspaper, it's too late to buy it. Why? Because other people have already pushed the price up. This principle applies more in investment selection than in any other industry."

• "If a stockbroker has mailed you a recommendation on a company, the chances are that he's mailed it to a hundred other people. So it's not as good a bargain as if you'd found it yourself."

As we've seen, these simple principles, and many others which may seem on the surface to be simple, often have profound implications. And to determine whether one of these principles applies to a company you're considering—or to determine how it applies— will probably take a great deal of research and study.

But what Templeton is saying is that it's important, in the midst of all this hard work and in-depth analysis, not to miss the forest for the trees. In other words, you might become a genuine expert on a series of small companies on the American Stock Exchange through Templeton's detailed methods of quantitative analysis. But if you were concentrating on this area in your search for bargains at the time this book was being written, Templeton would say you're missing the boat. You're getting entangled in the complexities of research, and forgetting a simple principle: Buy what others are not buying.

"It's much more difficult to find a bargain among small companies on the American Stock Exchange today," Templeton explains. "That type of stock has been popular in recent years, and security analysts have been searching through all the stocks on that exchange. So the chances of an American Stock Exchange stock being overlooked are not as great as they were eight years ago."

Templeton, by the way, is now focusing his search on the bigger companies listed on the New York Stock Exchange. Specifically, here's the way he's thinking in the autumn of 1982: "We don't ever ask ourselves, 'Shall we buy big companies or little ones?' or, 'Shall we buy American companies or Japanese?' We just search every day by keeping in mind the simple question, 'Where is something selling for a tiny price in relation to its true value?'

"And at present we're finding the answer to that question among the big companies. Take Mobil, for example, one of the world's very largest companies. At 24, it's selling for less than one third of what it could liquidate for. And it has a cash yield of 8.5 percent, which is roughly 50 percent greater than average stock yields. Not only that, it's selling for less than five times earnings, when the average stock in America now is seven times earnings. Also, the average stock in Japan is twenty times earnings. And this is just one illustration of how we are thinking at this point in time."

But it's an excellent illustration of how the simple principle of bargain-hunting always takes priority over detailed research. Or perhaps more accurately, it's an example of how Templeton always puts the simple principles first and then organizes his in-depth studies around them.

These ten principles, which we've been considering over the past three chapters, constitute the practical, investment side of the Templeton Touch. In a way, they can best be summed up by an overriding principle that Templeton often refers to when he advises: "Build your brick wall from the bottom, never the top."

By this he means it's important to lay a systematic groundwork for your vocation or avocation as an expert investor—before you ever start to commit significant sums of money on the stock market. "It's amazing to me how many people want to start out being important without doing the work that's necessary to become important," he says. "If you try to move too quickly, before you're ready, it's like a mason who starts to build a brick wall, but who lays the top bricks first. Obviously, if he does that, the wall is going to fall down!

"What you should do, instead, is to prepare yourself by study and observation—by watching other people, by reading and by practice that will enable you to become a real expert. If you come to know more about a particular subject than anybody else, then you're on a solid foundation. And that's the first brick in your brick wall. From that point, you add other bricks on top and on each side, so that gradually you build a solid brick wall—which is a successful and fruitful life.

"But if you don't—if you aren't willing to lay that foundation— then you are likely to be one of those people who go through life frustrated and upset and beset by feelings of inferiority. You don't have to go through that! All you have to do is be willing to do the work. Be willing to spend the hours and the concentration to build those foundation bricks on the bottom. Then the wall of your life will stand up and be a protection and a support for you until you die.

"I've seen any number of people—dozens, even hundreds— whose lives have been one failure after another, simply because they were unwilling to lay those first foundation bricks. But you can avoid this sad end if you'll just build your brick wall from the bottom, never the top."

Even as Templeton gives advice like this, it's natural to wonder: "Isn't there something else that explains his incredible success? Isn't there some other essential ingredient that we've overlooked?"

And the answer is, yes, there is another important ingredient in the Templeton Touch—one which may be the most significant of all. The problem in describing it is that it's not as easy to grasp as some of the practical, straightforward principles we've discussed so far. This other element—which may be called the "intuitive factor," for want of a better term—has such unusual ramifications that it deserves an entire chapter of its own.

8

The Intuitive Factors in Successful Investing

John Templeton is one of the hardest and most efficient workers in the field of investing. But all the hard work, careful quantitative analysis, shrewd bargain-hunting techniques, self-discipline and other business qualities only carry him up to a certain point: They prepare him for that final step that makes him one of the world's greatest investors—the exercise of good judgment in deciding which stocks to buy and which to sell.

The effectiveness of this final phase in his work depends on what might be called "intuitive factors." These qualities arise from deep within his personality and are based on a unique mixture of inherent traits, background influences and learned techniques. The hard work and practical preparation provide a springboard from which he leaps into the realm of creative insight. The solid foundation of his research gives him the freedom to understand concepts and industry relationships that remain out of reach of most other people—primarily because they aren't as well prepared.

With Templeton, the intuitive factor also merges into the spiritual realm. Prayer, meditation, "retreating" from the hullabaloo of the financial community, a willingness to share material goods—these are all elements that are present in one way or another in Templeton's decision-making and his disposition of the wealth he acquires.

But to understand how this intuitive dimension of John Templeton's mind works, it's necessary to do more than merely describe his views in the abstract. This side of his personality has roots deep in his childhood and has developed through a variety of concrete events throughout his life. So now let's take a brief excursion into the mind of John Templeton and try to understand those spiritual and psychological qualities that make him the kind of investor he is.

In an earlier chapter we learned that John's mother, Vella Templeton, had a strong influence on her son's spiritual development—especially as she created a home environment that focused on the Unity School of Christianity. In fact, this unusual spiritual movement's impact on Vella—and, through her, on her children—was decisive in helping to transform John, the grade-school entrepreneur, into an investment counselor with a world reputation for wisdom.

The Unity movement appeared in the late nineteenth century in Kansas City, Missouri. It arose from the thought and experiences of Charles Fillmore, a real estate entrepreneur, and his wife, Myrtle, a convert to the New Thought movement, which was similar in some ways to Christian Science.

Myrtle was attracted to the new spiritual undercurrents that were creeping across America because she had been healed of tuberculosis through a form of faith healing. Charles soon became as fascinated with the new use of spiritual forces as his wife, and they began to devote almost all their time and energy to understanding the new way of thinking and believing. Finally, in 1891, the Fillmores formulated their own special approach to Christianity and called it "Unity."

According to Charles S. Braden in his *Spirits in Rebellion,* one of the roots of the Unity movement can be traced back to the intellectual and spiritual ferment spawned by Ralph Waldo Emerson's Transcendentalism in the early nineteenth century. Another of the roots of Unity was the concept of "mental healing" advocated by Phineas P. Quimby, a New England clockmaker who became a self-trained hypnotist, healer and religious philosopher. The New Thought movement of the mid-nineteenth century grew out of the thought of many ministers and authors.

Transcendentalism, Quimby's philosophy, and New Thought were rather amorphous movements that interacted freely with one another and depended more on the writings of individual thinkers than on creedal statements of faith. But some generally held, distinctive features of the new American spiritual trends were:

• Man is essentially divine, or at least God is immanent in man's basic instincts and thought patterns.

• Intuition and prayer are a basic source of knowledge and reality, in addition to revealed authority like the Bible and ancient scriptures of other religions. Also there was a belief that God continues to reveal Himself to those who seek.

• The right view of reality and the universe is an idealistic one: In other words, human beings and their institutions can always be changed for the better through prayer and love.

• The idea of healing physical infirmities through divine power gained in popularity.

Christian Science, under the guidance of Mary Baker Eddy, arose from this spiritual caldron in 1866. And about twenty years later, the Unity School of Christianity appeared on the scene, using much of the terminology of New Thought and Christian Science, while at the same time displaying some distinct differences in approach and belief.

The Unity movement spread throughout the country during the late nineteenth and early twentieth centuries, as Charles Fillmore wrote and published prolifically. He mailed his books, booklets and magazines to Christians of every denomination during the late nineteenth and early twentieth centuries. In fact, one of the features of the Unity movement was that its adherents were encouraged to remain in their own churches, even as they learned to use Fillmore's interpretation of Christianity. Charles and Myrtle did not want to found a new church but to remain among the existing churches so that they could witness to their personal understanding of the power of love and prayer.

As the Unity School of Christianity reached out to far-flung cities and towns, one of the communities that it touched was Winchester, Tennessee. And one of the individuals who became deeply impressed by the Fillmores' beliefs and arguments was Vella Templeton.

Some of the beliefs that Vella studied in the Unity literature included:

• Truth is one—not even Christianity has a monopoly on it. Or as Hugh D'Andrade puts it in his book *Charles Fillmore:* "Unity regards the essence of all true religion as One."

Fillmore, who had studied various Eastern religions, like Hinduism and Buddhism, wrote in his first book, *Christian Healing:* "The perfect-man idea in God-Mind is known under various names in the many religious systems. The Krishna of the Hindu is the same as the Messiah of the Hebrews." And on another occasion he said: "I have taken the best in all religions and brought them all together in the light of Jesus Christ's teachings."

• Religion should be more concerned with man's physical health —especially with ways that positive control of one's thoughts can bring about vitality and healing.

• Material success and wealth should flow naturally from personal spiritual growth and progress. Charles Fillmore expounded on this topic in detail in his book *Prosperity,* published in 1936.

• Unity is the opposite of dualistic concepts that spirit and matter are separate, John Templeton says. The Unity School of Christianity believes that matter is only a manifestation, or "outpicturing," of the ongoing creative reality which they call God. Like Transcendentalism and the New Thought movement, the immanence of God in Unity thought approached a form of pantheism or, in Templeton's case, "panentheism." (Pantheism holds that the universe as a whole is God, while panentheism is the belief that the physical world and universe are a part but only a small part of God's being.)

• In a way reminiscent of Christian Science, the identity of Jesus was divided into two parts: (1) Jesus, the historic person; and (2) "the Christ," the divine principle or spiritual identity, which is the essence of every human. The distinctive thing about Jesus, according to Fillmore and the Unity movement, was that he was the only perfect man who had developed his "Christ consciousness" to the highest degree.

Fillmore and the Unity School *did* tend to be more Jesus-centered than the New Thought or Transcendentalist movements. But their views still created serious problems for many traditional Christians. For example, scholars from mainstream Christian traditions have pointed out that the Unity view of Christ's nature tends to detract from his deity: In other words, if the divine "Christ principle" in Jesus was just part of the divine that was in every person, then it couldn't be said he had a special God-nature that was different from that of every other human being.

But Charles Fillmore cared little for promoting a comprehensively consistent belief system. "His dogma was to avoid dogma," Templeton says. In fact, Fillmore stated explicitly that he always reserved the right to change his mind. Some of the ideas he threw out to his public caught on, and some didn't. For example, he sometimes mentioned the Eastern concept of reincarnation, and some of his followers accepted this belief. Now, almost all his followers reject it, but they still regard themselves as part of the Unity School philosophy. "Never in any Unity magazine or book can you find any criticism of any church or any person," Templeton says.

One of the best-known later religious leaders who was influenced by the Fillmores and their Unity movement, as well as by the New Thought thinkers, is the noted Christian preacher of success through positive thinking, Dr. Norman Vincent Peale. In fact, he acknowledged his debt to Unity and New Thought literature in a conversation with Professor Charles S. Braden for Braden's book *Spirits in Rebellion.*

For example, Peale, to illustrate a positive-thinking point in his *Guide to Confident Living,* quoted approvingly from Charles Fillmore's book *Prosperity:* "Do not say that money is scarce. The very statement will scare money away from you. . . . Do not allow one empty thought to exist in your mind, but fill every nook and corner of it with the word plenty, plenty, plenty."

So this is the kind of spiritual force that had crept into the Templeton household, especially into the thinking and convictions of Vella Templeton. And young John, though not particularly religious himself at the time, began to read *Weekly Unity,* a Unity School publication, at about age nine. As a result, he absorbed into his own mind and soul many of the thought patterns of Unity and of his mother's individualistic approach to spirituality. This influence has continued, as Templeton has read Unity magazines and books regularly during the past sixty years.

But it took many years—and a number of rather dramatic experiences, some tragic, or nearly so—for Templeton's own spiritual sensitivities to become sharpened. When he was seventeen years old, for example, he experienced his closest personal brush with death. "It was on a trip to California in 1929, when my mother, brother and a friend of ours were camping out near an ocean beach. This friend, Jimmy Grizzard, and I got up early, before the rest of the others, and went swimming in the ocean. But what we didn't know was that there was a strong undertow in that part of the ocean at that time of day.

"When we started to swim back and tried to put our feet down, we found we were in deep water. We swam and swam toward shore, but didn't get anywhere. In fact, we kept drifting farther out. After a long time—about a half hour of trying to swim back— we saw we weren't going to make it, and we were very tired. So we started shouting for help. But we got more and more tired, until finally we didn't have the strength to rise above the waves. We were really in bad condition. The waves were washing over us every few seconds, and we were really getting desperate.

"Then, all of a sudden, when we thought we couldn't stay afloat, somebody appeared nearby in a rowboat. It was one of the lifeguards, who had apparently heard our cries for help, but we didn't see him until he was within about ten feet of us.

"This fellow picked us up and took us back to an infirmary where they managed to get the water out of us. They kept us there for three or four hours, until we had completely revived."

Although Templeton doesn't believe this experience was the most important incident in his spiritual development, "it really did make me feel that God had protected me and that He had saved me for a purpose," he says. "Very often, perhaps a few dozen times in later life, I thought maybe God had some reason why He kept me here."

But during the next twenty years Templeton regrets that, for the most part, he neglected his personal spiritual development.

"From the time I was at Yale until twenty years later, I gave too little thought to spiritual matters," he recalls. "All through that twenty years I regarded myself as a serious Christian and a child of God. But I got an increasing feeling of being held back, an increasing feeling of a need to change my life-style or to change my goals. The things that were real and important, such as spiritual matters, were getting squeezed out by working so hard to become the best in my profession. I didn't have many friends who even talked about religion—not at Yale, nor at Oxford, nor in my investment-counseling business."

Materially speaking, of course, things were going rather well for Templeton during this period. He had bought his own investment-counseling company in 1940 for five thousand dollars, and after the usual slow start for a new professional firm, his personal assets began to increase. He had about thirty thousand dollars when the war broke out in Europe in 1939, and that had risen to about one hundred and fifty thousand dollars when he bought Vance Chapin & Company a couple of years later. He changed the name of the firm to Templeton, Dobbrow & Vance, Inc., and eventually his business interests diversified to the point that he was managing a group of mutual funds with scores of employees and hundreds of clients.

But then, just when everything seemed to be going just right, tragedy struck. In February 1951, Templeton's wife died in a highway accident when they were touring Bermuda on motorbikes.

"I had three young children," Templeton recalls. "I didn't know how to be a mother to them, but I had to try. I couldn't spend all day with them because I was in the midst of trying to build a business and earn a living. So I asked one of our two servants, Rozella Battles, to become the governess for the children. After the first few days, I found that the best thing to do was to go back to work, to fill my mind with my business. It was much better to keep my mind full of other things than to ponder over what had happened."

This tragedy was magnified, in a way, because his mother had just died a few months before, in September of 1950. In less than one year the two most important women in John Templeton's life were gone, and he was thrown back as never before upon his own spiritual resources.

But unlike many people who have undergone dramatic conversion experiences as a result of tragedy, Templeton's inner life wasn't immediately altered. Instead, he began a slow, gradual movement toward a more intense interest in religious things. And this movement coincided with other important developments in his personal and professional life.

For one thing, in 1954 he, Donald M. Liddell, Jr., Antonia Pis-

tey and other partners founded the Templeton Growth Fund and
thus launched the enterprise which was to become the most successful investment vehicle in modern history. On a more personal
level, he married Irene Reynolds Butler in December 1958. John
and Irene lived on the same street in Englewood, New Jersey, and
they had met casually at neighborhood parties. But they didn't really get together until John's youngest son, Christopher, became
friends with Irene's younger child, Malcolm.

Christopher, then age six, liked Irene so much that one day he
phoned her and said, "May I come to see you after school?"

"Certainly," she said. "Come and have tea with me."

After Christopher had finished his tea and cookies with Irene,
he looked at her and told her, without any beating around the
bush, exactly what was on his mind: "If you ever think of getting
married again, will you please consider my father?"

Somewhat disconcerted, Irene answered that she would. Several
years later, Christopher's dreams were realized. His father and
Irene became engaged, and all five of their children were given
roles in the wedding. John had three—John, Jr. (or "Jack," as he
is known), the oldest; Anne; and Christopher, the youngest.
Irene's elder child is a daughter, Wendy, and her son is Malcolm.
Irene is the daughter of the deceased Mr. and Mrs. Percival Tyn-
dale Reynolds of Boston and Philadelphia.

Unquestionably, John and Irene are close. She has supported
him in his spiritual pursuits, and in that regard Irene says, "Nothing gives me more joy than to help people find God in the way
that they understand." She is active in the Christian Science
Church, and for the twenty-three years they have been married,
John stresses, she has been an inspiration to him in his efforts to
encourage progress in religion.

To solidify their relationship in the early years and make sure
that all the children now regarded themselves as members of one
family, John and Irene planned an eight-week trip for the family
across Europe in 1959, the summer after they were married. And
in a manner reminiscent of a television situation comedy, they put
the kids in charge. To make matters even more interesting, they
invited three of the children of John's brother, Harvey, to accompany them.

Each of the eight youngsters was assigned a specific role of authority on the journey: For example, Jack was given the responsibility of taking care of everything to do with the hotels and deciding which cities they would visit. His cousin, Jill, the oldest at age nineteen, was put in charge of all the money. Wendy made all decisions about restaurants, and Anne was the historian and scribe. Harvey III, another cousin, was "boss" of the bus in which they traveled; Handly, the third cousin, was in charge of luggage. "Mac" (Malcolm) was the photographer for the trip; and finally, Christopher was put in charge of "no grumbling."

"He was picked for this job because at that age he was more likely to grumble than anybody else," Templeton says. "So if he noticed anyone complaining, he would have to point it out, and then the person caught grumbling would have to think up two pleasant things to say before he could take up his grumbling again."

The trip was a huge success, and John Templeton was, once again, a complete family man.

Then, as the nineteen-sixties unfolded, his spiritual and professional lives came together in a way that was to make him one of the best investors of this century. First of all, the group of mutual funds that he had established were doing quite well, and an insurance company offered to buy out John and the seven other shareholders. He had been having increasingly strong feelings that it was time for him to devote much more time to spiritual matters, and this opportunity seemed a good way to reduce his work load and focus his energies on religion. He wasn't quite sure what form those religious activities should take. But he knew that for his priorities to be right, a search for God and ultimate meaning in life would have to come first.

Or as he puts it, "I had spent my early career helping people with their personal finances, but helping them to grow spiritually began to seem so much more important."

But things didn't work out exactly as he had planned. He and Irene did finally select the Bahamas as their permanent home base —a place where they could live among people of deep spirituality in a setting of natural beauty that would be conducive to religious study and work. They built a permanent residence there with southern plantation architecture in the exclusive Lyford Cay Club area on the main island of New Providence. And in order to participate fully in helping his adopted country, then a British colony, he became a British citizen.

But as he says, he will always love his native land, "just as after a man takes a wife he still loves his mother more than ever."

Templeton immediately began to "practice what he preached" in his new home as far as promoting spirituality there was concerned. His Templeton Foundation gives scholarships to ministers in the Bahamas for study both in the Bahamas and at Princeton Theological Seminary. Also, each year the Foundation sponsors lectures in the Bahamas by the winners of the Templeton Prizes for Progress in Religion.

Another interesting concept his Foundation has introduced to the islands is Bible-verse plaques for the walls of all the Bahamas' schoolrooms. And in memory of Templeton's mother, Vella, the Foundation has established Templeton Theological Seminary, which is the first theological college in the Bahamas. Finally, Templeton serves as a director of Junior Achievement of the Bahamas, the Bahamas Development Corporation, and other corporations and charities.

When Templeton first moved to the Bahamas, he continued to manage one of his mutual funds, the Canadian-based Templeton Growth Fund, because under American laws, there was an 11 percent interest equalization tax imposed at that time on Americans who bought shares in it. The tax would have made it unattractive to sell the fund's shares to Americans—or at least that was the attitude of the insurance group that was buying the Templeton group of investment counsel companies.

So after beginning his new life in the Bahamas in 1969, John Templeton found himself spending about thirty hours a week overseeing his family investments and his one remaining fund, the Templeton Growth Fund, which has gone on to become the most successful mutual fund of all time. And he began to devote another thirty hours a week to religious and philanthropic work.

The performance record of the Templeton Growth Fund, which had been good for many years, turned out to be even better when managed from the Bahamas. "With the advantage of hindsight now, I think there are two reasons for this success," he explains. "One is that if you're going to produce a better record than other people, you must not buy the same things as the other people. If you're going to have a superior record, you have to do something different from what the other security analysts are doing. And when you're a thousand miles away in a different nation, it's easier to buy the things that other people are selling, and sell the things that other people are buying. So that independence has proved to be a valuable help in our long-range performance.

"Then, the other factor is that so much of my time in New York was taken up with administration and in serving hundreds of clients that I didn't have the time for the study and research that are essential for a Chartered Financial Analyst. And that was the area in which God had given me some talents. So now in the Bahamas I had more time to search for the best bargains."

But there was more to his increasing success than just greater opportunities for research. During this same period John Templeton also began to emphasize three "intuitive" factors in his investment activities. These were prayer, a "retreat" principle, and greater generosity and sharing of his wealth with others.

Intuitive Factor One: Prayer. When Templeton lists the things that have been most instrumental in his success as an investor, he always mentions prayer first.

"We start all of our meetings, including our shareholders meetings and our directors meetings, with prayer," he says. "If you start meetings with prayer, the meetings are more fruitful and more productive—you reach decisions that are more likely to help everybody concerned. There is less controversy if you begin a meeting with prayer. Or, as I like to say, 'Prayer helps you to think more clearly.' And in selecting investments, that is the most important thing—to be able to think clearly."

But what exactly is the Templeton approach to prayer?

"It goes back to my concept of God and His creative process," he explains. "God is infinite. Everything that exists in the universe and, much more, *beyond* the universe, *is* God. This means that the whole visible universe is really a small part of God and is itself a manifestation of God. By the word 'manifest' I mean that which is able to be known by a human being. So one little piece of God has become known to us through light waves and other things that enable us to perceive a few features of the universe.

"We ourselves are a recent creation of God and are a little part of God. If we realize this and try to bring ourselves into harmony with God, with the infinite Spirit—if we try to be humble tools in God's hands and become clear channels for His purposes—then we will be able to accomplish much more. And what we do accomplish will be more permanent and lasting.

"Whatever you do in life—whether you get married, bring a case to a law court, operate on a child, or buy a stock—you should open with prayer. And that prayer should be that God will use you as a clear channel for His wisdom and His love. You should open with prayer that every thought that enters your mind and every word and action that is taken will be in tune with what is right in God's purposes, for the benefit of all God's children and not just a selfish goal.

"And if you pray this way, everything you do following such a prayer is likely to be more successful. Your mind is not twisted by conflicts. You're less likely to disagree with your associates or do something you'll regret next year. So your decision-making will be improved if you try to bring yourself into contact with the Creator, into harmony with His purposes.

"If you make this basic effort to be in harmony with God and all of His children through prayer, then it's far more likely that anything you do in life will turn out for the best, including your selection of stocks. When we have directors or shareholders meetings or business meetings to discuss investment selections—whatever we do—we begin with prayer."

But how, exactly, does he pray for specific stock selections?

"We don't pray that a particular stock we bought yesterday will go up in price today, because that just doesn't work," he explains. "But we do pray that the decisions we make today will be wise decisions and that our talks about different stocks will be wise talks. Of course, those decisions and discussions are not always wise—no one should expect that when he opens with prayer, every decision he makes is going to be profitable. I believe more of them are good if you open with prayer than if you don't."

Templeton's most common way of praying—his personal technique for getting into harmony with God to make his investment decisions—is to pray simply, "Thy will be done." This approach helps him to empty his mind of all preconceptions and open himself up more completely to what he perceives as God's guidance. He says he tends to pray often throughout the day. And if there is a particularly difficult decision to make, he'll try to wait a day and spend some extra time in prayer before he acts.

"On those more important things, it is good to say, 'Well, I want to sleep on that and pray about it,'" he explains. "Then, I would work at it—collect all the information I need and give it all my thoughts. Before I go to sleep I say, 'God, I have done the best I can—now guide me in my decision.' And I'll go to sleep, and very often the next morning I've got a solution that is better than anything I could have thought of by myself the day before."

He also encourages his associates to participate in prayer—even when they are somewhat reluctant to get involved. "In public meetings I've found that it works better to select people and ask them to pray. This gets them to thinking along these lines. So my normal practice is that a day, or even an hour, before a meeting is to be held, I'll just pass by a friend and casually say to him, 'I'm going to ask you to open—or close—with prayer.' That gives him some time to think about it. And not only does it benefit the one who is praying, but also the people in the meeting don't have to listen to one person all the time. They listen to each of their friends pray, and that's much more beneficial than just having one person do it."

He has had people turn him down when he asks them to lead an investment discussion group in prayer, but this doesn't deter him from inviting them to participate in the future. "Many people are afraid to pray," he says. "They are just unable to utter the words. But if you keep asking them, some of them become able to do it. I've often said to a friend, 'Would you open with prayer?' And he'll say, 'Oh, please, no!' But then six months later I'll say, 'Well, *now* would you be able to open in prayer?' And he'll say, 'Yes, I will!'

"I have also had people write me and say they think it's a mistake for me to mention prayer in my public meetings because they don't believe there's a God. But among the people that I actually work with—either in religion or in business—I can't recall a case when anyone said he didn't believe in God."

Templeton's emphasis on prayer is by no means something that sprang full-blown into his investment life right at the beginning. "It's increasing, still increasing," he says. "I must admit that for the twenty years when I was a worse backslider than at any other time in my life, we didn't open our investment meetings with prayer. So it's really been developing gradually, over the last twenty to thirty years."

In other words, his stress on prayer has coincided with the most successful performance period of the Templeton Growth Fund.

Skeptics may downgrade the importance of prayer in Templeton's investment selections. They may say that he was successful even before he began to pray regularly or inject prayer so openly into his business sessions. And they may further argue that he would have reached the same heights of achievement as an investor even if he had neglected prayer altogether.

But John Templeton definitely feels otherwise. He believes that his prayer life has given him a clarity of mind and depth of insight that have been decisive in his success. Of course, there's no way to resolve this issue here. The individual reader and investor must examine Templeton's style and record and determine for himself just how powerful and influential a force he feels prayer has been in Templeton's investment activity.

Much the same sort of subjective evaluation must be made of the second intuitive factor in his approach to investing—the "retreat" principle.

Intuitive Factor Two: The "Retreat" Principle. As has already been indicated earlier in this chapter, Templeton believes that one of the major factors that enabled him to improve his performance as an investor after he moved to the Bahamas was that he was able to get away from the high-pressure atmosphere of Wall Street and the major financial markets.

When Templeton started out as a professional investor, he felt it was essential to be in or near New York. There is more access to investment information there and also more opportunity to build a client base and to make extensive personal contacts in the field. But Templeton never enjoyed New York. So after the initial purpose of establishing himself had been achieved, he began to look for a climate and neighbors more compatible with his personality.

The community can be a key element in helping a person make the best use of his native gifts, and such was certainly the case with Templeton. But it's important to note that he didn't move too soon. He got all he felt he could out of his work in New York, and then pulled up stakes and found a location where he could use to best advantage what he had learned.

And for Templeton that geographical setting was one that enabled him to strike a harmonious balance between hard work and unpressured reflection, between intense study and a state of repose in which that study could most easily bear fruit. The ideal setting for him was the ultimate "retreat" (the religious term for the practice of withdrawing from the world to contemplate God and matters of the Spirit). In other words, the best place for John Templeton to rise to his position as one of the world's greatest investors has been the sun, sand and tropical beauty of the Bahamas.

"When my wife and I were looking for the best place to live, one of the questions we asked was, 'Where can we carry on our work in the most pleasant surroundings?' " he recalls. "All my life I've enjoyed the open air, and especially the flowers, ocean beaches and clear water of the tropics. We were attracted very strongly to ocean beaches, and now that we live here we are surrounded by three ocean beaches. So I use every opportunity when I can get away from routine work and telephones to take a briefcase full of papers and sit in the shade on the beach. There I concentrate either on security analysis, or on religious reading or study. I find it's an excellent place to work. You can work with greater concentration there than you can in an office or in a home."

But even though that time for reflection and solitude on the beach is quite important for Templeton, the actual quantity of time he can spend there each day is rather limited. "I spend, at most, an hour a day at the beach thinking and doing my work," he says. "There are too many other demands on my time to spend any longer. But I do it almost every day I'm not traveling, and that turns out to be about one hundred and fifty days a year. It's a very pleasant time of withdrawal, and the interesting thing is that it seems to be productive, too, in terms of producing good overall results for our mutual funds. To be able to work with the sand and ocean surrounding me seems to help me to think in worldwide terms."

Now, one reaction to Templeton's practice of spending time in reflection, away from all the demands of an office, may be:

"That's just great, for a rich guy like Templeton. He's able to choose his favorite spot in the world and live and work there. But what does his choice of home have to say to me?"

It's true that very few, if any, part-time investors have the time or the means to take off regularly to ruminate on a tropical beach. But the underlying principle here is much more important than Templeton's particular life-style. After preparing himself thoroughly in the more hectic environment of Wall Street, he discovered that to reach his greatest potential he had to introduce into his life a withdrawal period, a time apart from all other investors—a "retreat" time, if you will.

Therein lies the key lesson for all other investors: They can do well if they work hard, learn the techniques for searching out bargains, and follow all the other practical principles that have made Templeton a superior performer in his field. But to reach the peak it's helpful to withdraw periodically. During these "retreats" the individual should let what he's learned sink in and give his mind the opportunity to roam freely and creatively. John Templeton does this on the beaches of the Bahamas, but others can do it anywhere they can find a reasonable amount of solitude. In any case, though, it seems essential somehow to set aside time for reflection.

Intuitive Factor Three: Greater Generosity and Sharing of Your Wealth with Others. John Templeton began the practice of "double-tithing," or giving away to charities 20 percent of his earnings, when he was in his late thirties. That was about the time when his mother and first wife died, and also the time when he became more sensitive to the religious and spiritual aspects of life. In later years he contributed even more of his income to various worthy religious causes, including the Templeton Foundation Program of Prizes for Progress in Religion. The annual prize, plus expenses, now amounts to more than $350,000 a year. After he dies, the Templeton Foundation and Templeton Religion Trust will have more than enough capital to carry on this program of prizes permanently.

There are many interpretations of the possible implications of this kind of generous giving. Some might refer to the biblical principle that "the more you give, the more you'll receive." The specific references that support this idea would include the following:

• "Bring the full tithes into the storehouse, that there may be food in my house; and thereby put me to the test, says the Lord of hosts, if I will not open the windows of heaven for you and pour down for you an overflowing blessing." (Malachi 3:10, RSV)

• ". . . give and it will be given to you; good measure, pressed down, running over, will be put into your lap. For the measure you give will be the measure you get back." (Luke 6:38)

• ". . . he who sows sparingly will also reap sparingly, and he who sows bountifully will also reap bountifully . . . for God loves a cheerful giver." (2 Corinthians 9:6, 7)

In Templeton's case, then, it might be argued that his greatest material success came after he began, paradoxically, to give more of his wealth away. He believes firmly in the spiritual principles from the Christian Scriptures and readily attributes at least a part of his material success to the power of those principles in his life.

But aside from the spiritual dynamic of generosity giving rise to greater wealth, there is another dimension to the significance of sharing one's investment profits with others. John Templeton believes in investing his money not only in properties that will generate other money, but also in causes and projects that further religious research and what he perceives as the will of God on earth. By directing large portions of his funds into these channels, he magnifies the enjoyment and sense of meaning he derives from earning profits on his investments. And that sense of satisfaction stimulates him still further to plunge back into his investments and make even more money—money which he can, in turn, plow back into the great causes of his life.

So what we have here is a kind of gaining-giving-gaining-giving cycle, which feeds on itself and leads to ever greater investment profits and ever greater charitable gifts. Throughout the entire process, Templeton believes his own feelings of gratitude and his sense of purpose in life have grown as well. To emphasize the benefits of thanksgiving, John and Irene have not sent Christmas cards for the past twenty years; instead, they have mailed to friends pictures of their family with inspirational messages of thanksgiving on Thanksgiving Day.

In Templeton's life the greatest charitable gift of all has been the Templeton Foundation Prize for Progress in Religion—a subject about which much more remains to be said. But before we leave the topic of investments, let's let John Templeton himself give us in his own words a final overview of his investment principles.

9

The Time-tested Maxims of the Templeton Touch

These are the twenty-two key guiding principles that Templeton says have enabled him to become one of the world's greatest living investors. These points are expressed in his own words, and they serve as a kind of summary statement of the Templeton Touch. Some of these have been discussed in depth in previous pages; others are relatively new nuggets of wisdom; all are maxims that the savviest investors should keep in mind as they decide where to place their money.

1. For all long-term investors, there is only one objective— "maximum total real return after taxes."

2. Achieving a good record takes much study and work, and is a lot harder than most people think.

3. It is impossible to produce a superior performance unless you do something different from the majority.

4. The time of maximum pessimism is the best time to buy, and the time of maximum optimism is the best time to sell.

5. To put "Maxim 4" in somewhat different terms, in the stock market the only way to get a bargain is to buy what most investors are selling.

6. To buy when others are despondently selling and to sell when others are greedily buying requires the greatest fortitude, even while offering the greatest reward.

7. Bear markets have always been temporary. Share prices turn

upward from one to twelve months before the bottom of the business cycle.

8. If a particular industry or type of security becomes popular with investors, that popularity will always prove temporary and, when lost, won't return for many years.

9. In the long run, the stock market indexes fluctuate around the long-term upward trend of earnings per share.

10. In free-enterprise nations, the earnings on stock market indexes fluctuate around the replacement book value of the shares of the index.

11. If you buy the same securities as other people, you will have the same results as other people.

12. The time to buy a stock is when the short-term owners have finished their selling, and the time to sell a stock is often when short-term owners have finished their buying.

13. Share prices fluctuate much more widely than values. Therefore, index funds will never produce the best total return performance.

14. Too many investors focus on "outlook" and "trend." Therefore, more profit is made by focusing on value.

15. If you search worldwide, you will find more bargains and better bargains than by studying only one nation. Also, you gain the safety of diversification.

16. The fluctuation of share prices is roughly proportional to the square root of the price.

17. The time to sell an asset is when you have found a much better bargain to replace it.

18. When any method for selecting stocks becomes popular, then switch to unpopular methods. As has been suggested in "Maxim 3," too many investors can spoil any share-selection method or any market-timing formula.

19. Never adopt permanently any type of asset or any selection method. Try to stay flexible, open-minded and skeptical. Long-term top results are achieved only by changing from popular to unpopular the types of securities you favor and your methods of selection.

20. The skill factor in selection is largest for the common-stock part of your investments.

21. The best performance is produced by a person, not a committee.

22. If you begin with prayer, you can think more clearly and make fewer stupid mistakes.

10

A Prize Worth
More than Money

As John Templeton's spiritual sensitivities increased through the nineteen-sixties and early seventies, he began to look for some significant, concrete way to express his religious orientation. The result was the Templeton Progress in Religion Prize, which was first awarded to Mother Teresa of Calcutta in 1973. It has since been given to religious leaders across the entire spectrum of belief, from the late Sir Sarvepalli Radhakrishnan, President of India, a Hindu, to Protestant evangelist Billy Graham.

The particular nature of the prize, which carries with it a cash award that is the largest of its kind (slightly more than the amount of the Nobel Peace Prize or any other award), is in many ways a reflection of the personal values and religious views of Templeton himself. He decided it should be larger than any other prize in order to say to the world that progress in religion is more important than progress in any other area or even in all other areas combined.

Templeton unequivocally describes himself as a dedicated and enthusiastic Christian, and his affirmation of basic Christian tenets, such as the full and unique deity of Christ, certainly puts him in the company of many who identify themselves with the Christian church. Religious Heritage of America elected him for its "Churchman of the Year Award," and Religion in Media for its "Golden Angel Award." Also, his position of leadership in various Christian organizations and institutions, such as the chairmanship of the board of Princeton Theological Seminary, tends to reinforce his identification with the mainstream Christian tradition. He serves on the Board of Managers of the American Bible Society; and his honorary degrees include Doctor of Divinity as well as Doctor of Laws and Doctor of Humane Letters.

The underlying premise in Templeton's personal theology is that in order to make progress toward a fuller understanding of God, man must be "humble" before the divine presence—or assume a posture of personal and intellectual inadequacy in light of God's infinite superiority to us. In this way, he stresses in his 1981 book *The Humble Approach,* human beings will be more likely to remain open-minded and more receptive to all sorts of revelations and discoveries on the spiritual frontiers of life. And the more open-minded they are as they pursue various forms of "religious research," the more progress they can make in coming a little closer to understanding God. "All God's children should love each other and listen to each other," he says.

Templeton's open-ended approach to religious knowledge positions him as more of a religious "universalist" than many in the historic Christian traditions. That is, he tends to see significant elements of truth in all religions and denies that Christianity has a corner on spiritual truth.

On the other hand, he also sees the religions of the world as functioning in a kind of "spiritual free-enterprise system," where loving competition forces each to do its best to gain a better understanding of God. In the arena of religious competition, Templeton feels that Christianity has the most to share with others, and this is one of the reasons he wholeheartedly supports evangelists and missionaries. He doesn't foresee any likelihood of Christianity falling behind the other faiths in terms of spiritual progress and enlightenment.

The concept of spiritual free enterprise should not be taken to mean that Templeton advocates any sort of syncretism, however, or a one-world religion where all present faiths are combined into a unit through the affirmation of a set of doctrinal lowest common denominators. That would undercut his fundamental conviction that more progress tends to be made when there is a rich variety of belief in the world. And it would result in a sort of "religious socialism" where individual freedom is stifled. In other words, in spiritual as well as in economic matters, John Templeton adamantly favors a relatively unrestricted atmosphere in which each of us "joyfully seeks to give to others his greatest treasure, which is his knowledge and love of God."

Finally, Templeton's view of God's nature and His relation to the universe is what is called "panentheism," or "all *in* God." He says this term distinguishes his position from pantheism, which says that "all *is* God." In the tradition of Ralph Waldo Emerson's Transcendentalism and much of the New Thought movement—including the Unity School of Christianity—Templeton believes that God is the underlying reality of everything, and everything is a little part of God. But he also believes that God's nature goes infinitely beyond the material manifestations that make up our visible universe. "Scientists are multiplying the evidence that the unseen is vastly greater than the seen," he says.

He, in effect, denies a distinction between the Creator and His creation, except that the Creator is infinitely more than His creations. As a result, he sets himself apart from the biblical tradition of a Creator who made the universe and also living creatures, including human beings, who are "good" and yet still separate from their Maker.

John Templeton's personal beliefs are always evolving and growing, he says, just as were those of Charles Fillmore, the founder of Unity. But the state in which those beliefs now exist and the constant movement that characterizes them are reflected in a broader way in the Progress in Religion Prize that he has established.

For example, when he first began to consider awarding a prize for religion, he thought it should be limited to Christians. But as he discussed the matter with his close associates and with representatives of large religious bodies, like the World Council of Churches, "it seemed more loving to include every child of God." And that decision, of course, was quite consistent with his own universalistic tendencies.

The initial impetus for the prize came when Templeton became concerned that many of his friends—especially the best-educated ones—seemed to be neglecting religion.

"They thought of religion as uninteresting and old-fashioned, or even obsolete," he recalls.

In contrast, some of the work Templeton was doing with religious organizations like the United Presbyterian Church Commission on Ecumenical Mission and Relations and Princeton Theological Seminary, called his attention to "the marvelous new things going on in religion. There were new churches being formed; new schools of thought arising; new books being written on spiritual matters; new religious orders being established; and new denominations appearing. And I thought, how wonderful it would be if my friends could hear about these things and read about them. They couldn't help but be uplifted and inspired if they could just be informed about what was happening."

The general tone of press coverage around the world seemed to ignore or even run counter to the religious movements that Templeton was noticing. So he decided to try to do something about it, and gradually an idea formed in his mind.

"I struggled with this issue for a long time," he said. "Finally, I decided that, because I had limited resources and was just one person, the best I could do was to try to single out some of these wonderful people and help them to become more well known—not so much for their own benefit, but for the benefit of people who might be inspired by them."

He thought of the Nobel Prizes as an example and decided to establish the same sort of award for religion. So a clause was included in his will stipulating that, after his death, his trustees would award a prize for progress in Christianity. And there the matter rested for four or five years.

"But then I began to realize that it was a mistake for me to leave the assets for later use, because 'later' might be a long, long time away," he continued. "I might live twenty years, and in that case the world and my living friends would miss out in hearing about these wonderful religious movements and people."

So he sought advice from Dr. James McCord, the President of Princeton Theological Seminary, and also from Lord Thurlow, the former governor of the Bahamas. After discussing the matter with them, he decided to go ahead with the program of prizes while he was still alive.

"It was during those formative years, particularly when talking with friends in the World Council of Churches, that we decided also that it would be a prize for progress in religion of all types, so no child of God would feel excluded," Templeton says.

The next step was to put together a panel of distinguished judges, and that task was accomplished over the next three years. "The reason we have elected distinguished judges is that the fame of the judge helps the prizewinner to be heard of more widely," Templeton explains. "And the more people who hear about the awardee, the more people there are who will be uplifted and inspired by his work. So we decided on a board of nine judges. There would be a rotation system, with each judge serving three years and three new judges coming onto the board every year."

Templeton also decided that there should be a minimum of one judge from each of five major religions, and at least half of them would be nonprofessionals in religion. "In this way, they would be more likely to be receptive to new ideas," he says. "Also, there would be variety in continents, sexes and races. In everything, we wanted rich variety."

The next step in setting up the procedure for the prize was to decide how the nominees would be selected and voted upon. "We took the national annual report of my own church and found there were twelve people who, between them, would know if any Presbyterian had done something entirely original. Then we took each of the other Christian denominations and also all the sects of other religions and went through the same process of selection."

The result was two thousand people who were designated as official nominators for the prize. Next, the Foundation elected a board of sixty advisers from all continents to make suggestions about improvements that should be made in the selection procedures. And finally came the question of who should make the first presentation.

"In my early conversations with Lord Thurlow and Dr. James McCord, both of whom were selected to serve on our first board of judges, I said, 'If we had a really famous person to award the prize, it would be beneficial to a much larger number of people,'" Templeton recalls. "With the help of Lord Thurlow's friend, Sir Robin Woods, then Dean of Windsor, His Royal Highness Prince Philip, husband of the Queen, graciously consented to award the first prize in 1973 and has continued to do so each year."

So now the stage was set to move ahead and award the first
Templeton Foundation Prize for Progress in Religion.

"In the ten years we've been giving the awards, we've received
about four hundred good nominations," Templeton says. "And
there were many that came in that first year. This prize is not
something you can apply for. It comes to you because other people
think you're producing good fruit. Also, the prize is not given for
something a person has done recently. It's for something that he or
she did in an original way throughout a lifetime."

In addition to eliminating self-nominations, the Foundation
staff tries to identify and remove nominations that are clearly the
result of lobbying efforts. "We don't find any appreciable amount
of lobbying, but there have been a few cases. Of course, it's not
unusual to have five different people nominate the same person,
but that's not necessarily lobbying, especially not when they've
acted independently."

After the officers of the Templeton Foundation gather together
the better nominations, they spend as much time as they can collecting additional information about the nominees. They examine
what the candidates have written and what's been written about
them. When possible, they also visit the candidates, talk with
them, and then write up a report on their accomplishments and
background. In this way, each year about thirty completed investi-
gations of qualified candidates are submitted for consideration by
the judges. "We mail these out in many batches each year, and the
judges consider them at their leisure," Templeton says. "The
judges don't meet together, mainly because they are so busy and
famous that it would be impossible to get them together at one
time and place.

"Then, usually in December, we narrow the field down to about
five who have received the highest number of votes from all the
judges," Templeton explains. "The Foundation sends these names
to all the judges so they may vote on the five finalists. The one
who gets the highest tabulation in the voting will become next
year's recipient."

The announcement of the winner has been made in recent years
in a ceremony at the United Nations in New York City about the
first of March. Then, in May, the winner receives the prize and the
cash award from Prince Philip, usually in a private ceremony at

Windsor Castle or Buckingham Palace. The prizewinner also gives a lecture at Guildhall in London before eight hundred invited guests and dignitaries. This is followed by a reception at which the guests meet the recipient and some of the judges.

The panel of judges constitutes, as Templeton has indicated, a kind of "who's who" of laity and clergy from all the world's religions. As of this writing, the present board of judges includes:

The Dalai Lama, the religious leader of Tibet.

The Most Reverend Stuart Blanch, Archbishop of York, England.

Senator Orrin Grant Hatch of Utah, a member of the Church of Jesus Christ of Latter-Day Saints.

The Honorable Philip M. Klutznick, former President of the World Jewish Congress and Secretary of Commerce under President Carter.

Her Royal Highness the Grand Duchess Josephine of Luxembourg.

The Right Reverend Michael Mann, Dean of Windsor and Domestic Chaplain to Queen Elizabeth.

The Right Honorable Lynden O. Pindling, Prime Minister and Minister of Economic Affairs of the Bahamas.

Dr. Nagendra Singh, a member of the International Court of Justice at The Hague.

Former judges include:

Mr. P. N. Bhagwati, a judge on the Supreme Court of India.

The Reverend Dr. Eugene Carson Blake, former General Secretary of the World Council of Churches, U.S.A.

Professor Suniti Kumar Chatterji, National Professor in India in the Humanities and past President of the Senate of Bengal.

His All Holiness Demetrios I, Ecumenical Patriarch, Turkey.

Mr. Masakazu Echigo, Buddhist layman, President of C. Itoh Company, Japan.

Her Majesty Fabiola, Queen of the Belgians.

Mr. Charles Rickert Fillmore, Chairman of the Board of Directors and President of the Unity School of Christianity.

Former President Gerald R. Ford.

Senator Mark O. Hatfield of Oregon, a leading member of the Senate Prayer Breakfast Group.

Dr. Inamullah Khan, Secretary-General, World Muslim Congress, Pakistan.

Sir Muhammad Zafrulla Khan, former President of the International Court of Justice at The Hague, Pakistan.

Dr. Margaretha Klompe, the first Dutch woman to become a cabinet minister.

Sir Bernard Lovell, Professor of Radio Astronomy at the University of Manchester, England.

The Reverend Dr. James I. McCord, President of Princeton Theological Seminary; President, World Alliance of Reformed Churches.

Mr. Yehudi Menuhin, violinist, England.

Sir Alan Mocatta, Judge of the Queen's Bench Division of the High Court of Justice, England.

The Lord Abbot Kosho Ohtani, Patriarch of the Nishi Hongwanji Temple, Japan.

Mr. Apasaheb Balasaheb Pant, former Indian Ambassador to Italy.

The Reverend Dr. Arthur Robert Peacocke, Dean of Clare College, Cambridge.

The Reverend Dr. Norman Vincent Peale, Minister of Marble Collegiate Church, New York City, and founder of *Guideposts* magazine.

Her Serene Highness Princess Poon Pismai Diskul, Thailand, former President of the World Federation of Buddhists.

Mr. Edmund Leopold de Rothschild, former President of the Bank of Rothschild, England.

The Right Reverend John V. Taylor, Bishop of Winchester, England.

The Right Honorable the Lord Thurlow, former governor of the Bahamas.

Mr. Leo Tindemans, former Prime Minister of Belgium.

The Right Reverend R. W. Woods, Bishop of Worcester, England.

As this list of notables shows, the Templeton Prize has benefited from the work of some of the most influential figures in religion and society in general. Increasing numbers of people are becoming aware of what the prize is all about, as these well-known individuals make the award, often to equally well-known winners. And in those cases where the winners have not been so well known, their lives and efforts to further their faith have often received considerable public attention as a result of the publicity surrounding the prize.

So the ultimate purpose of John Templeton—to spread the word about major new spiritual developments throughout the world—seems well on the road to accomplishment. And his entire family has joined in the effort. John's brother, Harvey; his wife, Irene; and all five of their children are trustees of the Templeton Foundation. The children include:

• One son, Dr. John M. Templeton, Jr., is a pediatric surgeon at Children's Hospital in Philadelphia, and his wife, Josephine, is an anesthesiologist in the same hospital. They have two daughters, Heather and Jennifer.

• Daughter Anne is a general surgeon in Casper, Wyoming, and is the wife of Professor Gail Zimmerman.

• Daughter Wendy and her husband, Eugene Brooks, live in Delray Beach, Florida, and have three boys—Sander, Colin and Cameron.

• Son Christopher is in the horticulture business in Jamestown, North Dakota, and is the sponsor of a Christian charismatic community for troubled young people.

• Son Malcolm Butler lives in Columbia, South Carolina, and is a vice president of Century Capital Company, a real estate investment company.

But now let's turn from the man Templeton to those men and women who have won the Templeton Foundation Prize. He has chosen to broaden his personal commitments from helping people increase their wealth to helping them learn more about religion, and there is no doubt that to some extent he has succeeded. But specifically, who are these people placed in the spotlight by the prize? And to what concrete uses has the award been put?

In many ways these questions are just another way of raising the issue that has challenged John Templeton perhaps more than any other throughout his life: "What is the best way to achieve progress—and especially progress in religion?"

How to Live a More Abundant Life

A Practical Guide to Spiritual Progress from the First Ten Recipients of the Templeton Foundation Prize for Progress in Religion

11

What Is Spiritual Progress?

We live in a century which, for the most part, has been characterized by a widespread belief that in the long run things are going to get better and better. In other words, during most of the past eighty years—despite certain relatively short periods when a mood of negativism has prevailed—many people have tended to assume that, increasingly, good things are going to happen to them and their culture.

For example, people often believe:

• they are going to acquire more of the material goods of life;

• technological and scientific advances will continue to make life easier for greater numbers of people;

• the general trend of politics is for governments to become more responsive to the needs of the greatest number of people;

• more diseases are going to be stamped out; and

• man's inhumanity to man is going to become less and less of a problem.

Of course, even the most optimistic individuals will acknowledge that some limits should be placed on this belief in an upward spiral of human improvement. As this book is being written, for example, the national and world economies are in the doldrums; unemployment is high; the talk of widespread depression is rife; and wars and rumors of wars punctuate the international scene.

But as the Preacher says: "There is nothing new under the

sun." (Ecclesiastes 1:9) There have always been relatively bad times and "doomsayers" in every age, and negative thinkers have been listened to more closely at some times than at others.

The negative words may come in an economic guise—from those, for example, who argue that we are on the verge of economic collapse. Or the cautionary note may wear a religious cloak —as when we are warned that the end of the world is near and the Second Coming at hand. Or, again, the most strident warnings of doom may be political—from those who contend that our government is falling apart or that World War III is pending. And in especially bleak years, several or all of these pessimists may take center stage for a time.

These negative voices must be listened to carefully because no one knows precisely what the future holds, and any one of the would-be prophets may be sounding a note of truth. But even when the doomsayers have been most powerful and persuasive, they haven't been able to obliterate a belief that has set the basic tone of long-term historical attitudes in the West for centuries—a belief in the ultimate triumph of good and the long-range progress of mankind in all fields of endeavor.

Of course, the advocates of progress can be as realistic as anyone else. Those who believe strongly in progress will usually acknowledge that we'll always face some economic, political or social setbacks. Also, they'll agree that there are certainly ultimate global threats that seem destined to hang over us for the foreseeable future, such as the danger of a nuclear holocaust. Finally, even when there's nothing specifically terrible to point at, the advocates of progress are as sensitive as anyone to the fact that a maddening and sometimes immobilizing aura of uncertainty often hangs over all our human plans and efforts.

But in the minds of the historical optimists, this bad news is only a temporary interruption of the long-term, good news that history is unveiling for our benefit. They tend to think of the future more in terms of a gradually ascending spiral, rather than a flat plane or a downward slide to some new dark age.

In more specific terms, this belief in progress seems to exist on at least four conscious levels: (1) scientific or technological improvement; (2) economic improvement; (3) political improve-

and an implicit action plan to help us get there. The main difficulty, though, is that these assumptions about spiritual progress often exist primarily in the subconscious. In other words, many people are quite aware of what they believe about the future prospects of the economy, politics, social values, science and technology. But the spiritual assumptions and moral values that underlie and help to shape those beliefs about the future are often buried deep within.

Despite the fact that assumptions about spiritual progress may not be so obvious, they carry tremendous power. For example, our underlying beliefs about what constitutes spiritual progress give us a way of distinguishing between upward historical movement, and movement which is merely sideways or even downward. So our subconscious assumptions about spiritual progress enable us to determine the direction in which our technological, economic, political and social forces are carrying us.

But perhaps the most important element in the concept of spiritual progress is an assumption that deep inside each individual is the capacity to improve morally and to begin to think and live more in harmony with a *good* universal value system. Some believe this spiritual orientation of each human being is the result of some instinctive kind of altruism; others are convinced it is derived ultimately from God "who is creating us," as Templeton puts it. But whatever the source, the internal moral structure in each person is the vehicle which motivates him—and many others like him—to try to further progress in the world at large.

Of course, there's nothing particularly new about these attitudes. As a matter of fact, many historians and theologians think the seeds of our present belief in progress lie far back in the Judeo-Christian roots of the Western religious heritage.

For example, British historian Herbert Butterfield has said: "I think . . . that progress . . . is itself the work of Providence, and is part of that providential order, part of that history-making which goes on almost, so to speak, above our heads. For men did not just decide that history should move—so far as concerns certain particular matters—either as an ascending ladder or as a spiral staircase as though it were a growing plant. They did not say to themselves: 'Now we will establish progress.' On the contrary, they looked back and discovered to their amazement that here ment; and (4) social improvement. In other words, any given in dividual may be optimistic over the long haul that:

• new scientific discoveries and technological advances wil make his life easier in various ways;

• his material well-being and economic status will improve;

• the political system in which he lives will become more responsive to his needs; and

• civil and human rights will spread increasingly around the world.

Now, of course, as we've already seen, it's easy to take exception to all these generalizations. Sometimes, for example, it may seem that the economic pie we must divide among the world's peoples is so severely restricted that there is no potential for future growth. At other times we might seem to be confronting an economic recession—or even a depression—with no light at the end of the tunnel. Or disillusionment with political leadership may be so great that there seems little hope that a real statesman will come along and save us from our sorry state. Finally, any given minority group may feel their efforts to gain more rights and opportunities have run into a blind alley.

But despite the negative voices which are raised periodically, many polls consistently show a mood of optimism about the typical individual's attitude toward the prospects for his own future. For example, Ben J. Wattenberg, in his *The Real America,* stresses that Americans in the early nineteen-seventies expressed great optimism in almost all national polls that the future outlook for them *personally* was quite rosy.

Some of the surveys did indicate that Americans thought life was getting worse; but that attitude mostly applied to the "other guy," not to the individual being polled. These same optimistic attitudes seem to have continued pretty much intact in polls conducted since Wattenberg's study.

But this mood of optimism about the future couldn't exist at all were it not for some generally accepted assumptions about another, less visible kind of progress—what might best be called "spiritual progress."

Simply stated, spiritual progress involves a group of moral and spiritual assumptions about where history *should* be taking us—

was a thing called progress which had already been taking place. . . ." (*Christianity and History*)

Butterfield argues that some kinds of knowledge do have to be learned from the beginning again with each era—such as the most creative art and literary forms. But other kinds of knowledge, such as those that are rooted in science and technology, can be *accumulated* from generation to generation. He also believes that this accumulation moves *upward* and serves as a foundation for the improvement of human society only because of an underlying divine guidance—the active presence of God in the movement of human history. In other words, if God weren't present, our accumulation of information would be *merely* accumulation and might actually do us more harm than good. Templeton Prize recipient Ralph Burhoe has expressed essentially the same idea in his writings.

But Butterfield also offers one word of caution about this idea of an upward spiral in human improvement. He warns that if human beings start operating outside of God's will—or in disobedience to the divine laws in the universe—then God's judgment may fall on them. Or to put it in Butterfield's own words: "Providence therefore does not guarantee the progress—does not promise an ascending course no matter how human beings behave."

How well does Herbert Butterfield's view of progress square with traditional religious thought?

First of all, the belief in an active divine presence at the helm of historical developments is quite consistent with the historic Jewish and Christian faiths. Also, his idea of an inner spiritual development, which is a precondition for outward social, political, economic and scientific progress, seems quite consistent with historic Jewish and Christian thought.

For example, in the Old Testament God is presented as the God of history, the One who says through His prophets: "I will shake the heavens and the earth and the sea and the dry land; and I will shake all the nations. . . ." (Haggai 2:6–7)

Also, even as He worked in history, God's favorable treatment of His Chosen People, the Israelites, always depended on their obedience to Him—especially, on how well they kept His covenants. Sometimes, as individuals, they went astray and violated the principles of conduct and worship that He had laid down through various prophets and spiritual leaders. And at those times they ran into political and social difficulties. The final result might be their defeat in battle or even eventual captivity by their enemies. On the other hand, when they obeyed God and His commandments and anointed leaders, they prospered materially, politically and culturally.

A similar kind of relationship between outward social progress and inner spiritual development is evident in the New Testament. There is a tremendous emphasis in the Gospels on the importance of fostering an inner spiritual growth that will, in turn, be manifested in helping others.

Jesus, for example, says in the heart of the Sermon on the Mount (Matthew 5:48): "You, therefore, must be perfect, as your heavenly Father is perfect."

In other words, in some way the moral and spiritual perfection of God must be incorporated into imperfect human nature. In fact, in this same sermon He goes on to urge upon His listeners an approach to personal morality and interpersonal relationships that would seem impossible without the presence of God's power inside the individual. For example, there is a strong implication that unless a person experiences some dramatic, life-changing *inner* spiritual progress, he will be unable to follow such a radical call to *outward* moral action as, "Love your enemies and pray for those who persecute you. . . ."

St. Paul picks up this same theme in his letters. In writing to the church at Philippi, he sounds the call to move toward moral and spiritual perfection, even though he admits that he himself hasn't quite arrived yet: "Not that I have already obtained this or am already perfect; but I press on to make it my own, because Christ Jesus has made me his own. Brethren, I do not consider that I have made it my own; but one thing I do, forgetting what lies behind and straining forward to what lies ahead. I press on toward the goal for the prize of the upward call of God in Christ Jesus." (Philippians 3:12–14)

But perhaps the best biblical statements that combine inner spiritual development with outward progress can be found in the letter of James, the great leader of the early church in Jerusalem: "What does it profit, my brethren, if a man says he has faith but has not works? Can his faith save him? If a brother or sister is ill-clad and in lack of daily food, and one of you says to them, 'Go in peace, be warmed and filled,' without giving them the things needed for the body, what does it profit? So faith by itself, if it has no works, is dead." (James 2:14–17)

This combination of growing inner convictions and concrete expressions of those inner convictions in good works has always been a basic principle of Jewish and Christian religious expression. One of the main reasons that inner spirituality and personal commitment lead naturally to an emphasis on improving personal relationships and getting involved in social and political action is that these two faiths are *historically based.*

In other words, the God of the Jews had a certain historical plan and destiny in mind for them, and all His interactions with them were designed to see that this plan was fulfilled. The God of the Gospels continues to focus on the overriding importance of certain historical events—especially the death and resurrection of His Son—as part of the divine plan of salvation for mankind. So the God of both the Old and New Testaments is a God of history, and what happens in the daily events that constitute history really makes a difference to Him.

This historical orientation of traditional Judaism and Christianity has often been mentioned as one of the main features that sets them off from many of the world's other major religions—especially Eastern faiths like Hinduism and Buddhism. In the Eastern religions, there has tended to be an emphasis on inner perfection and a de-emphasis on social and political action to change the course of history. Historical progress, in the sense that Western nations have come to know it, doesn't have deep religious roots in the meditative religious traditions of the East.

But in recent years, as the world has become more of a "global village" through sophisticated forms of communication and travel, a notion of progress has also seeped into the spiritual thought of the East. The result has been the relatively recent development in Hindu and Buddhist cultures of a belief that inner spiritual progress can spur concrete, visible progress in the world at large as well. Now, to see precisely how the belief in progress has become perhaps the most important single social and political assumption in advanced nations throughout the world, let's continue with our brief historical excursion.

Despite the strong Christian foundations that support a belief in progress, Western cultures haven't always functioned as though progress in social, political, moral and scientific matters were possible. In fact, after the fall of Rome, the West went through the many centuries of the so-called Dark and Middle Ages when knowledge was preserved and revered among a small intellectual elite. But what human beings knew and learned wasn't taking them anywhere in any practical sense. For the most part, they weren't *using* what they knew to make life better or more comfortable for the average person than it had been the century before.

But then a change in expectations about the potential of human knowledge occurred. Modern-day historians trace our present beliefs in progress back to the seventeenth-century English scientist-philosopher Francis Bacon.

In *The Advancement of Learning* and *The New Atlantis* Bacon argued very pragmatically that the gathering of knowledge shouldn't be just an abstract exercise that occurs in ivory towers among the world's intellectual elite. He believed that all new information and knowledge should be put to work for the betterment of mankind. This may seem like a sensible, even obvious position to take today; but it was anything but obvious in Bacon's time. In fact, it was considered downright radical in some circles.

But the idea that knowledge should have practical uses to improve the world caught on during the ensuing centuries until it became the major article of faith among Western nations. Here's how historians R. R. Palmer and Joel Colton put it in *A History of the Modern World:*

"The idea of progress is often said to be the dominant or characteristic idea of European civilization from the seventeenth century to the twentieth. It is a belief, a kind of non-religious faith, that the conditions of human life become better as time goes on, that in general each generation is better off than its predecessors and will contribute by its labors to an even better life for generations to come, and that in the long run all mankind will share in the same advance."

After Bacon, many philosophers took up the banner of progress and introduced it far and wide to leading thinkers and political leaders of many nations. The French political theorists Turgot and Condorcet helped transform the belief in progress into a full-blown philosophy of history by identifying historical stages through which they believed each society would move.

As a matter of fact, Condorcet's faith in progress was so strong that he could continue to affirm it, even when he was in great personal danger in the wake of the French Revolution, which he had supported. It seems that his independent attitudes had caused other leaders of the Revolution to suspect his motives, so he was forced into hiding. Finally, he was caught and imprisoned, and soon afterward was found dead, either from exhaustion or poison, on the damp floor of his cell.

But individual tragedies like this didn't deter advocates of progress from their shining vision of what they saw as the ultimate future of mankind. Later philosophers, like the nineteenth-century English utilitarian philosopher John Stuart Mill, expanded still further upon the theory by suggesting that "the human mind has a certain order of possible progress." Mill also suggested that this innate human propensity toward mental and moral progress is reflected in the gradual improvement of various human institutions.

George Sabine, former professor of philosophy at Cornell University, has concluded that for Mill it must have been "possible to show by far-reaching comparisons that the growth of mind is correlated with the advancement of civilization. . . . In nineteenth-century Europe it was possible, perhaps even plausible, to entertain the expectation that political institutions everywhere would be liberalized by a process of gradual evolution." (*A History of Political Theory*) In a related development, as John Templeton frequently notes, the concept of *economic* progress through free enterprise was pioneered by the great work of Adam Smith in 1776, called *An Inquiry into the Nature and Causes of the Wealth of Nations.*

Eventually, these ideas linked up with Charles Darwin's theory of evolution, which saw progress occurring in the world of biology. And philosophers like Herbert Spencer began to express theories of historical progress in terms reminiscent of biological evolution.

So, in practical terms, what had now happened to the idea of progress?

In effect, many philosophers and many average people by the

nineteenth century had begun to think that progress would take place on two levels—in the human mind and spirit, and in society at large. And those two levels of reality were intimately connected with one another.

As one generation of thinkers accumulated knowledge and passed it on to the next generation, progress took place in one sense on an intellectual or cerebral level. But inevitably this inner progress had outward manifestations, as the great practical minds of each age applied ivory-tower theories to real-life situations. So technological inventions proliferated; social systems became more sensitive to the needs and rights of broader groups of people; and life in general seemed to improve for everybody.

Perhaps the most enthusiastic national forum for advocating the gospel of progress in this era was the United States. And the most impressive and influential spokesman was the American philosopher and essayist Ralph Waldo Emerson.

Harvard's Pulitzer Prize-winning historian Oscar Handlin describes Emerson's approach and thought this way:

"Few Americans were more carefully listened to than he. For years he traveled a national circuit, working over the subjects he later published as essays. In the process, he gave the German idealism and the English romanticism that had stimulated him a distinctive American cast.

"Emerson's vision perceived a mystical unity in the universe. Every object of nature had not only the particular form of its own being but was also a part of the transcendent oversoul called God. In this pantheistic communion, every man shared a spark of the divine. The natural impulses that animated each in his free actions were divine; and self-reliance was God-reliance. Man had only to turn to nature for reason and faith.

"[For example, Emerson said:] 'Standing on the bare ground,— my head bathed by the blithe air, and uplifted into infinite space,— all mean egotism vanishes. I become a transparent eyeball. I am nothing. I see all. The currents of the Universal Being circulate through me; I am part or particle of God.'" (*The Americans*)

Handlin concludes that for most Americans in Emerson's nineteenth-century milieu, "Progress, in fact, was a law of history. . . . In arriving at this faith in man's ability to perfect himself, the Americans had come a long way from the time when they had conceived themselves helpless sinners in the hands of an angry God. They had recast, in terms of their own experience, the ideas derived from the Great Awakening and inherited from the enlightenment of the revolutionary period. The expansion and growth of a half-century were the manifestations of their own power and merit; the painful deficiency in what had thus far been achieved was the unfinished business of the future. The assurance of indefinite progress alike gratified the successful and consoled the failures."

This belief in progress gathered steam in the United States throughout the nineteenth century, and a variety of reform movements, utopian communities and other outward expressions changed the face of American society. Europe experienced a similar kind of intellectual, social and political transformation in the wake of a general acceptance of the possibility of progress of all sorts, in every field. And as technological developments have enabled the East to meet the West in the twentieth century, the gospel of progress—of the potential upward mobility of mankind in all fields of endeavor—began to have practical effects from India to Japan.

So the idea of progress, despite its deep roots in the Western spiritual tradition, gradually became a secularized belief which, on the surface at least, seemed only vaguely related to spiritual concerns. But the spiritual underpinnings have always remained at the foundation of our belief in the possibility of human improvement. Even when religious and spiritual values aren't mentioned, they are always hovering in the background when the issue of progress is raised.

For there to be progress, there must be a set of standards to follow, a goal to shoot for, a set of ultimate values to affirm. Otherwise, the upward movement that constitutes human progress becomes random, aimless motion. And the human dramas, which make up the events of our daily lives, as they are grouped in larger expanses of historical periods, become meaningless babel, with no discernible order or structure.

For there to be progress, there must be an underlying assumption about what progress is. There must be some value system to determine whether or not things really are getting better. And it's at this point that spiritual progress joins hands with all other kinds of progress and contributes ultimate meaning and direction to the entire historical process.

Some of the most significant recent efforts to highlight the importance of spiritual progress in our lives have been made not by a professional philosopher, historian or theologian—but by a businessman, John Marks Templeton. In his book *The Humble Approach,* he has called for research efforts to study and enhance spiritual progress, efforts which he believes should be undertaken with the same urgency that we pursue research in scientific fields.

And Templeton has put his money where his convictions are—by establishing the Templeton Progress in Religion Prize, the world's largest cash award of its kind, to recognize those individuals who are doing the most to promote spiritual progress in the world today.

So far, there have been ten winners of the Templeton Prize, and they come from a variety of backgrounds and religious traditions. But as different as they are, the life of each of the winners reflects these four basic principles, which seem to lie at the heart of any understanding of spiritual progress.

• *Spiritual progress has both inner and outer dimensions, which promote personal and social improvement.* In other words, there first must be some spiritual development—some growth with God or other ultimately meaningful principle—going on *inside* an individual or group of individuals. And at the same time, this inner growth or maturity must motivate or inspire the individual or individuals to do something constructive which improves or has the potential to improve mankind at large.

• *Spiritual progress is grounded in history.* In a sense, this is a corollary of the first principle, because the outward expression of inner spirituality must take place in an historical setting. To qualify as an example of progress, an action taken, a book written, or an idea formulated must have some meaning beyond itself—some practical, beneficial implications for people involved in the stresses and strains of everyday life.

• *Spiritual progress involves something which is new.* In some cases spiritual progress may come about through a new expression of an old revelation from God. In other cases spiritual progress may result from what is perceived as a new divine revelation—though not necessarily one that is inconsistent with former revelations. But unless a person's or a religious movement's contribution in some way furthers human understanding of God, it can't rightly be regarded as progress. In this regard, Templeton is fond of the biblical quotation, "By their fruits ye shall know them."

• *Spiritual progress often includes or is combined with progress in other fields of endeavor.* For example, new ways of helping the poor and underprivileged in our world may be both a form of social work and an expression of spiritual progress. Or combining scientific insights with an increased understanding of God may constitute a form of spiritual progress.

Of the first ten winners of the Templeton Prize whose lives and beliefs will be described in the following pages, eight come from Western religious traditions and two from the East. All seem to believe in some form of spiritual progress, and their inner beings and outward works testify eloquently to this belief.

But the time has come to move beyond abstract definitions to the specific, living people of our own day whose work serves as the best definition of spiritual progress. So now let's take a closer look at one of the most striking spiritual figures in the world today, a woman whose very name brings to mind images of the ultimate in spirituality—Mother Teresa of Calcutta.

12

Mother Teresa of Calcutta
The Secret of Finding Abundance in Poverty

True spirituality is often punctuated by paradox. So we are told, you must "lose your life in order to save it." Or you must "give in order to receive." Or you can only find true freedom in a life that is totally under the sovereignty of God.

These are all statements or concepts that run contrary to common sense; yet from the perspective of spiritual growth, they are all true. In other words, they are classic paradoxes that reflect the profundity of an advanced experience with God.

From this same metaphysical mold comes one of the major discoveries of Mother Teresa of Calcutta: There is an abundance of benefit and meaning in abject poverty. Christ's love—indeed, Christ Himself—is to be found literally and in overwhelming measure in the lives of the poorest of the poor.

But the full significance of this insight wasn't something that registered on Mother Teresa overnight, nor did her understanding of the poor come into full flower at the very beginning of her life of service. On the contrary, the development of her beliefs took time. She had to undergo a long period of inner progress in order to reach a spiritual level that gave her the power to accomplish her great outward, concrete acts of mercy.

She was born Agnes Gonxha Bejaxhiu, the child of Albanian peasant parents, in Skopje, Yugoslavia (Serbia), in 1910. And during her early youth her prospects for future greatness of any sort seemed rather limited. But then the spark of her future mission was lit as she began to listen intently to letters read at her school from a Yugoslavian Jesuit who had embarked on missionary work in India.

Little Agnes was so inspired by what she heard that she volunteered to work for the Bengal Mission. Soon, in 1928, she was sent to Loreto Abbey in Ireland to meet with the Loreto Sisters, who were involved in missionary work in India. They accepted her for their overseas work, and she was immediately sent off to a novitiate in Darjeeling, India—at the tender age of eighteen.

The next twenty years involved a long period of preliminary spiritual groundwork. The time span is reminiscent of the more than one decade of preparation St. Paul says in Galatians (1:17–21) that he spent in Arabia, Syria and other parts of the Middle East before he embarked on the major thrust of his evangelistic ministry. During her own period of spiritual apprenticeship, the young Yugoslavian nun taught geography in a Calcutta high school; took her final vows; and finally, in 1946, experienced a divine direction into her present work while on a train bound for Darjeeling.

On that train Mother Teresa, in trying to find God's will for her life, received a "call within a call"—a divine summons to devote her entire being as a nun to serving the poorest of the poor. Reflecting on the inner spiritual growth which had led up to that personal revelation, she said: "The whole life is a preparation to go home to God. The whole life, except when we misuse our lives and commit sins. So to the young person just beginning with God, I would say, take one thing at a time. One thing at a time. There is no hurry."

And clearly *she* was willing to wait—for nearly two decades— until God's special message came to her. "But still, we must really put our whole heart and soul into doing what God has given us a chance to do," she says, cautioning that waiting for God doesn't mean becoming idle or doing nothing. "The apostles had to give up everything immediately and go. So with us—it's the same thing. When Christ comes into our life and asks us to do something, we also must go. That's why that man [in the New Testament, Mark 10:17–22] who was so rich was not able to give up everything and follow Christ when Christ asked him to 'follow me.' But this is what young people are looking for—they want a challenge, where they can give up everything."

So it was a spiritual challenge that Mother Teresa herself was seeking, and she found that challenge after emerging from intense prayer on that train that was chugging toward Darjeeling. "You cannot take any step without prayer," she says. "Then, as the fruit of prayer, God will show you the way. But if we really want to love God, we have to give Him a free hand. He must be able to use us without consulting us. We must lay down no preconditions, absolutely none."

This total openness to revelation and complete submission to the divine will resulted in an obscure young nun's becoming perhaps the major living symbol of Christian charity throughout the world. And the events which established her spiritual leadership came swiftly after her experience on that Indian railway.

The year 1948 was a watershed in many ways: Desmond Doig, in his *Mother Teresa: Her People and Her Work,* notes that at that time she began to live outside the Calcutta cloister and to spend her time working with the "poorest of the poor"—those unfortunates who were dying or at least were considered beyond human help. She also started wearing her now familiar white sari with a blue border; and she became an Indian citizen.

The next year, her first follower, a Bengali girl named Subhasini Das, joined her. And the year after that, 1950, her congregation of the Missionaries of Charity was approved by the Roman Catholic Church, and the Mother House was established in Calcutta.

But even as she blazed new spiritual trails in helping the poorest Indians and other indigents of our time, her own inner spirituality was developing simultaneously. She didn't become a "living saint," as she has often been described by the press, in just a few months or even a few years. It's taken a lifetime, and the process of growth is still continuing.

For example, now she has an incredibly deep empathy for the poor. She actually believes that Christ Himself is present in the people to whom she ministers. Her biblical basis for this belief is her literal acceptance of Matthew 25:31–46, where Jesus says, in part: ". . . for I was hungry and you gave me food, I was thirsty and you gave me drink, I was a stranger and you welcomed me, I was naked and you clothed me, I was sick and you visited me. . . . Truly, I say to you, as you did it to one of the least of these my brethren, you did it to me."

But this sense of Christ's real presence in the poor, as intense as it is now, was not as well developed when she first embarked on her mission. "I have received much more from the poor than I have given to them," she explains. "Naturally, the feelings [of Christ's actual presence among the poor] have deepened. For example, when you read something, very often it doesn't go in straightaway, as you want it to. But with the second reading and maybe the third, each time you understand better and better.

"That's the way with the spiritual life also. You grow. You merely *accept* in the beginning. Then you keep on deepening by practicing it, living it, doing it. And you come to know that His words are not only words—they are Life. Because He has said, 'I am the Truth'—to be told. 'I am the Life'—to be lived. 'I am the Way'—to be walked."

This process of spiritual growth—of becoming more aware of the *real* presence of Christ in daily life—involves a paradox of sorts, because the deeper and more profound the Christian's faith becomes, the *simpler* it becomes as well. "We get confused with all that we hear and all that we see and all that we desire," she says. "But the mind of God is with the child—and that's what we're supposed to grow into. Becoming a child means *really* growing into the likeness of Christ!

"He became man for that reason—to show us how to become a child. So as we grow, we get the mind of Christ and let Him live His life in us. And the more Christ-like we become, the more people can look up at us and see only Jesus. They see Him in our actions, in the way we speak, in the way we pray, in the way we live."

So gradually Mother Teresa moved from a mere acceptance of what Jesus said about His real presence in the poor, to a deep belief in and feeling of that presence. "When you begin your work, you say, 'I'm doing this, Jesus—with you and for you I do it.' And then, I come close to the person, and I begin to touch him and I *know* that it is Jesus."

Finally, she concludes this insight with her characteristically simple—but always profound—logic: "It *must* be like that because

He cannot be seen, no? He has said, 'I was hungry, you gave me to eat. You did it to me.' But [sensing this actual presence of Christ is] a deepening, a growth. It doesn't come suddenly. First, you have to come to know the love, kindness, compassion and thoughtfulness of God. Then, the more you know Him, the more you love Him—and the more He is present with you. You *feel* that presence!"

This inner spiritual growth is what sets Mother Teresa apart from those who are doing good works in a secular context. "That's the difference between us and social workers," she says. "We may be *doing* social work, but we are not really social workers. We are real contemplatives in the heart of the world. We are with Christ twenty-four hours out of every day, as we feed the poor, buy clothing, take care of the sick, the dying and the crippled. That's what makes a contemplative. And by being with the poor, we have learned to pray better."

Indeed, prayer and her belief in the real presence of Christ in the Eucharist, or Holy Communion, are cornerstones of her personal spiritual power. And they are the key personal resources that give her powerful motivation and "staying power" in her difficult work, no matter how demanding the mission may become.

"We learn to pray by praying," she explains. "You see the need for prayer often during the day, and then you take the trouble to pray. Prayer enlarges the heart until it is capable of containing God's gift of Himself. Also, as you pray, you should read the Gospel and meditate on it—talk it over with God, conversationally. Prayer is a way of meeting God face-to-face."

But what is her specific approach to this prayer life, which has been so crucial in sustaining her and guiding her in her work?

"As for the amount of time to spend in prayer, we have nearly two hours during the morning Mass, Holy Communion, and meditations," she says. "Then, in the evening we have one hour of adoration and the blessings. During adoration, we kneel for a whole hour in silence. That's a wonderful thing, after a full day's work, to come face-to-face with Him alone. Very good. Only we do it as a community; we do it together. But in silence. It's a wonderful gift of God to us."

But always the seeds of action are present, even in these moments of silent contemplation. Or, as Malcolm Muggeridge quotes

Mother Teresa in his *Something Beautiful for God:* "The more we receive in silent prayer, the more we can give in our active life. We need silence to be able to touch souls."

Then it's evident that her private prayers and silent meditations give her a spiritual momentum which she nurtures by other kinds of prayers throughout the day. "During the rest of the day, we try to 'pray the work,'" she explains. "We do our work *with* Jesus, do it *for* Jesus, and do it *to* Jesus. If I do it with Him, if I do it for Him, and if I really believe that I'm doing it to Him, I can [be with Him in prayer] twenty-four hours each day."

This ability to sense the immediacy of Christ's presence in their work is perhaps the single most important factor that gives Mother Teresa and her sisters in the Missionaries of Charity their unique spiritual power. Just by being in contact with her is often enough to lead a person from abstract, dead religiosity into a heartfelt personal encounter with the divine.

One illustration of what may happen to a person who is close to Mother Teresa involved a young French girl who was one of their volunteer workers in Calcutta. A student from Paris University, she told Mother Teresa that she had been going regularly to Confession and Holy Communion for fifteen years—but had never found Jesus there.

"She said, 'Oh, I've found Jesus, I've found Jesus!'" Mother Teresa recalled. "I said, 'Where did you find Jesus?' And she said, 'I found Him in the home for the dying.' Then I asked, 'And what did you do for Jesus?' And the girl said, 'I found Him there in the home as I was doing the humble work, touching and loving those who are dying.'"

But Mother Teresa doesn't by any means suggest that it's necessary to go halfway around the world, to the slums of India, to find Christ among the poor. "I insist that you should find the poor in your own place, maybe in your own family," she says.

The greatest human need in Western nations, she continues, is "to know each other. If people know each other, they will love each other. And if you really love each other, you will do something for each other. I think the whole world is so busy that people have no time just to smile at each other.

"We all talk so much about the poor. But people have no time to look at the poor. To talk to the poor. Often, many don't even know where the poor exist. They would be surprised to know that they have a great many poor people right in their midst. For instance, there are the shut-ins that we have in New York and other cities. I think this kind of poverty is much greater than the poverty that I meet in Africa or India."

In particular, she explains, the poverty in the more affluent countries is "a hunger for love. There are persons who are left alone, unknown, unloved, uncared for, dying of fear and loneliness. We must come to know that we have the poor living right here, right in our own families."

For example, she says, "Maybe we have a lonely old father or an old mother. Or a crippled child or a mentally retarded child. Or we may have relatives in an institution who need tender love and care. Love always must begin at home. I think a lack of love and care in our homes creates a terrible kind of hunger. And one plate of rice or bread won't satisfy it. In the West there seems to be more of a poverty *inside* the person than on the outside."

So Mother Teresa believes in showing love first to those who are near to you—those who cross your path every day. And this means even the beggars on the streets of American cities, including those panhandlers who may use your money to buy a drink.

"Whenever we give, we give to Jesus," she explains. "He has identified Himself with the hungry, the naked and the homeless to make it possible for us to love God. After all, how can we love God if not through others? Jesus has given us an opportunity to love God in action—through these poor who approach us for money in our cities, these poor to whom we already owe deep gratitude for accepting our services."

But what if a panhandler really does use her contribution to buy a drink?

"I tell our sisters that I'd rather we made mistakes in kindness than work miracles in unkindness," she says. "Maybe that man will buy a drink. But then too, he may buy a piece of bread or pay for medicine for his child. We don't know. So I'd rather make a mistake than not to give at all. If someone approached me for something, I would always give it."

This, then, is Mother Teresa's basic philosophy of showing love to the poorest of the poor. It's a philosophy she applies regularly and consistently in her travels throughout the world. And it's a philosophy which has enabled her to discover abundance even in abject poverty—or as she might say, *especially* in abject poverty.

For Mother Teresa there is a kind of "divine logic" that makes showing love for the poor an absolutely necessary part of showing love for God. In fact, she doesn't think it's possible to show love for God without showing love for the poor.

"From a natural point of view, we all want to love God, and that is good," she says. "But *how* can we love God? Loving Him through words is not enough. So He has given us an opportunity to show love for Him in living action. He has made Himself the Bread of Life [in the Eucharist] to satisfy our hunger for love. And also, He has made Himself the hungry one [in our midst] so that we can satisfy His hunger for love.

"So there's that connection between the Eucharist and service to the poor. And the presence of Christ [in both] is definite because He has said so. It *must* be so. If He's going to judge us on what we have been to the poor, that Bible passage [Matthew 25] must be something real. It can't be only the imagination."

For Mother Teresa the commands of Christ to show love for the poor are certainly not a matter for the imagination. As she says, "Love for God is love in action," and she lives that principle to the letter, regardless of the fatigue that frequently overtakes her or the dangerous situations she encounters in furthering her mission.

For example, there was the time that she established a home for the dying in a building next to the Kali temple in Calcutta. The place she was using had been used by Hindu pilgrims to the temple at one time, but then it was taken over by various criminal elements and street people. Many of the Hindus who went to the temple didn't like the idea that this foreign nun was helping the poor, because they feared she would convert them to Christianity and perhaps aggravate the already difficult social problems in that area. So they "ran around and shouted," Mother Teresa recalls, and even threw things at her building.

But she and her sisters were unswayed in their dedication. And then something happened that completely changed the attitude of the people in that neighborhood toward her and her work. One day she noticed a sick man lying outside the temple, with a crowd gathered around him. As she moved closer she saw that it was a temple priest who was quite sick—in fact, it turned out that he had tuberculosis and as a result had been turned out of the temple.

"I picked him up and took him in when they wanted to throw him out," Mother Teresa said. "When we brought him in, he was cursing and shouting and blaming everybody. But then the man changed completely. After some time, as I talked to him, he became completely different. In fact, the other Kali priests used to come from their temple to see him, and they couldn't understand what had happened to make him so different. He did finally die, but he died a beautiful death. And he had received the blessing and the Sacrament."

After that incident, the fear that the local Hindus had toward this foreign woman and her strange religion dissipated and, as she says, "we became the greatest friends."

This sort of dramatic action has become a way of life for Mother Teresa. But now her work and outreach are not limited to India. She is likely to appear wherever there is tension, misunderstanding or violence between peoples, in an effort to promote love and peace.

For example, she went to Northern Ireland to try to promote understanding between Protestants and Catholics during the 1981 hunger strikes by Irish Republican Army internees at the Maze Prison outside Belfast. She also went to Lebanon to comfort the wounded and dying during the 1982 Israeli invasion of that country. Though she's already past seventy, she's on the road and in the air as often as a busy executive—but usually she carries only a paper bag or an equally small container as her "baggage."

Does she frequently get tired?

"Naturally," she replied, as she sank back wearily into an easy chair at a convent in Ballycastle on the northern shore of Northern Ireland. She had just appeared for a series of meetings at the interdenominational Corrymeela Community, which was trying to encourage better Protestant-Catholic relations even as the I.R.A. hunger strikes were tearing the society apart.

"The human body is human, no? But at the same time, 'praying the work,' visiting, talking—these are offerings to God. So being in His presence in the midst of my duties is not so exhausting. Some of our poor people have things to do that are much more tiring. They get up early in the morning and go to work without meals.

Or they stand in the road with nothing each day, hoping that somebody will give them work."

But earlier that day she had been under great physical pressure herself, as adults and children had crowded in around her, touching her and asking her questions. Didn't all the attention sometimes become overwhelming?

"I don't say anything because the more you say, the more attention you draw to yourself," she explained. "And if you accept everything people do to you, it passes off that much easier. But if you resent it or try to prevent it, then there are more questions, and more attention is drawn to yourself."

And how does she interpret the fact that they all want to crowd in and touch her?

"I don't know. Perhaps it's people wanting to show their love. And it's not only here. It's the same even with non-Christians. I think that people's love for the poor and awareness of the presence of the poor has grown tremendously. They often feel they cannot show love to the poor, but they still want to show love to someone. And since I represent, so to say, the poor, I think that's the connection. They begin with me. But then soon they want to feel the actual presence of the poor. They want to touch the poor, do something for the poor.

"I've become like a bridge between the rich and the poor."

As she sat there, so tiny and frail in this convent room, wearing a sweater over her sari to help ward off the cold, she seemed almost physically incapable of doing all she was doing. But that's a human evaluation; and Mother Teresa of Calcutta can't be understood in ordinary human terms. Perhaps the only way she can really be understood is in terms of the words of St. Paul, who wrote in Philippians 4:11, 13:

". . . I have learnt to manage on whatever I have. . . . There is nothing I cannot master with the help of the One who gives me strength." (The Jerusalem Bible)

13

Brother Roger of Taizé
A Study in Simplicity

The symbolism was almost perfect.

At a recent meeting of young people held in Rome—a meeting which included a prayer at St. Peter's with Pope John Paul II—Brother Roger, prior of the ecumenical Taizé Community in France, was scheduled to address some thirty thousand people gathered in three basilicas. He was also to have an audience with the Pope to discuss the work of Taizé and other serious ecumenical issues.

But he had something else on his mind—something that was just as important to him, in a way, as the weighty matters of the church. That "something" was a little girl, his goddaughter, who had been adopted into his sister's family when she was an infant.

The child was as dear to him as if she had been his very own. She called him regularly, saying, "Come and see me! Come and see me!"

When she learned that he was leaving for Rome, she insisted on going with him. Of course, there was no way that he could turn her down. And there was no way that she would let him out of her sight while they were on the road.

So as he spoke during the prayers at the Roman basilicas, he held his speech notes in one hand, steadied her with the other as she perched on his knee, and fought a losing battle trying to keep his glasses in place on his flat, straight nose.

She even clung to him as he went in for his discussion with the

Pope; and on that day an extra pair of little ears were privy to a papal audience.

The scene was reminiscent of Christ's teachings centuries earlier: "Let the children come to me, and do not hinder them; for to such belongs the kingdom of heaven. . . . Whoever humbles himself like this child, he is the greatest in the kingdom of heaven."

A child and a spiritual leader, side by side—the mental picture suggests the intimate connection between simplicity and profundity. It's been said that the greatest ideas are the simplest. The same thing can be said of great spiritual insights and the history-changing movements which arise from them. No matter how profound a spiritual concept may be—or how many complex, paradoxical ramifications it may have—at its core it's likely to be quite simple.

For example, take a seemingly simple statement from Jesus: "So whatever you wish that men would do to you, do so to them. . . ." (Matthew 7:12, RSV) On its face, this teaching may seem straightforward and obvious. Yet when a person begins to meditate on this command and tries to incorporate it in a practical way into his personal life, the implications become endless.

This interplay between the simple and the profound is characteristic of Brother Roger—or "Frère Roger," as he is called in French—and of the brothers of the Taizé Community. But for Roger, born Roger Schutz in Switzerland on May 12, 1915, things were not always like that. As a young man, the only reality he accepted, at least in his own life, was the complexity of the mind and the visible reality of science. He was an honest fellow, and honesty demanded that he accept as true only that which he knew from his own experience to be valid.

Yet even as Roger affirmed only the visible world in those days, he sensed that some sort of invisible world also had to exist—mainly because this immaterial realm was so real in the life of his maternal grandmother. "It had to exist because my grandmother was so honest and lived from her relationship with God," he said.

Also, both she and his father, a Protestant pastor, moved easily between Catholic and Protestant traditions and churches. As a result, the spirituality that he sensed in his household was in no way bound by narrow, denominational lines. God, if he existed, was obviously big enough to transcend the artificial walls erected by human beings.

So young Roger became a spiritual searcher who engaged in "deep questioning" about the nature of that second, invisible sphere of reality that remained just outside his personal knowledge. He read and pondered Pascal; and he listened intently during family readings of the history of Jacqueline-Marie-Angélique Arnauld, the seventeenth-century Abbess of Port-Royal, France. Port-Royal, under Mother Arnauld's direction, was a hotbed of Jansenism. And yet what interested Roger in the women of Port-Royal was not the Jansenism, which challenged papal authority, but the strength of their community life.

Roger was impressed because "those few women changed something in an entire period of history. Very often, a small number of women and men, dispersed throughout the world, have been able to shake up the historical determinism which seemed unavoidable."

His period of reading and reflection was intensified involuntarily when he came down with tuberculosis. And upon his recovery, he had moved a long way toward a more definite affirmation of Christian spiritual values. But it took a near-fatal illness of one of his sisters, Lily, who was about to give birth, for him to move more fully into a relationship with Christ.

It was the summer of 1937. Roger, who was then a rather reluctant theology student at Lausanne, had grave doubts about his personal spiritual position and his choice of profession. But Lily's illness brought all his inner turmoil to a head.

"With death so close, I wondered what I could say to God," he recalls. "So I took the words of a Psalm and prayed, 'I seek you—the depths of me seek your face.' I said this to God often, and that was all."

But it was also enough. Lily recovered completely, and Roger had rediscovered the meaning of prayer. It didn't involve any special feeling of "sentiment," however. "My family is very reserved, no sentimentalism," he says. But despite the lack of emotion, what had happened to him was undeniably an encounter with that "invisible world" that he had sought for so long.

Roger had no idea exactly where this discovery would lead him. And he didn't receive any special revelation about his future. He

just lived day by day and tried to grow closer and closer to Christ. This meant, first of all, becoming president of the Student Christian Federation.

Then, when the war broke out, the tests of his faith became more stringent: He resolved to find a large house that he could use to harbor refugees, and in 1940 he found just what he was looking for in Taizé, near Cluny. After considerable prayer, thought and consultations with friends in Switzerland, he bought the house—and settled into a life of severe danger in war-torn France. He managed to escape just days before the Gestapo, who had learned that he was helping Jews and other refugees, came in to occupy the house.

Then, in the company of three other young men, Roger began to live a communal Christian life in Geneva. But when liberation came to France in 1944, he moved back to Taizé with his spiritual brothers and established a simple rule of life, which J. L. G. Balado quotes in his *The Story of Taizé:*

"Throughout your day let work and rest be quickened by the Word of God.

"Keep inner silence in all things and you will dwell in Christ.

"Be filled with the spirit of the Beatitudes: joy, simplicity, mercy."

Some of the young men farmed in the fields, and all got together three times a day to pray in a chapel they had set up in the old house. Perhaps most important of all—and an indication of the direction their ministry would lead them in the future—they began to take in orphaned boys and developed a vital outreach to other young people in the area.

During the years that followed, the community grew, and in 1952 and 1953 Brother Roger formulated a "Rule of Taizé." Some of the salient features of the commitment the brothers made were: consecration to Christ and to service of the brothers within the community; renunciation of all individual ownership of property; communal holding of material goods; and celibacy.

The brothers also resolved to keep their independence by refusing all material gifts from outsiders and earning their own living. Today their income comes mostly from two sources: (1) a publishing program, with special emphasis on their own books; and (2) ceramic work, including pottery and stained glass.

Another distinctive feature of the Taizé Community is that the brothers come from various Christian traditions—including Reformed, Lutheran, Anglican, and Roman Catholic. They each remain a part of their chosen denominations, yet are still able to relate to one another in Taizé as fellow Christian believers.

One of the main reasons for the good official relationship between Taizé and the Roman Catholic Church has been Brother Roger's productive relationships with the Popes, and especially Pope John XXIII. He first met with Pope John in 1958, the day after John became Pope. The two men immediately established a warm friendship, in part because they both placed strong emphasis on a simple approach to the spiritual life.

"He was a man who dialogued with God," Brother Roger said. "That first meeting was very simple. He said, 'Bravo! Bravo for reconciliation!' It was a very free personal encounter. He was always joyful, and he lived in the present moment. He marked our life very, very much.

"With a rare generosity, he said, 'You are part of the church. The church is like large concentric circles, and you are part of the church.' And he said some very beautiful, strong words that I dare hardly repeat, they were so generous. Maybe one day, later.

"This man had such a wide vision of things. Pope John was, in a way, the man who brought us out of the Counter-Reformation. In 1958, he said himself, 'We no longer want to search who was right and who was wrong.'"

This ecumenical tone has continued in Taizé to the present day. And the lack of barriers between denominations is matched by the international flavor of the community. There are Taizé fraternities all around the world, including North and South America. In the community's church in Taizé, the Church of the Reconciliation, at least five languages are used in the services: French, German, English, Spanish and Italian.

As Brother Roger's personal faith and community experience have deepened, the simplicity with which he expresses spiritual truth has become more important. In other words, for him, the journey toward spiritual maturity—the inner progress toward a deeper understanding of God—seems to be a movement from complication and confusion to transparency and clarity. In a more general sense, it's also a movement from the troubles and anxieties

that weigh down the typical adult, to the carefree joy of child-hood.

Here are some of the most important personal spiritual traits and beliefs which have emerged from the inner journeys and out-ward experiences of Brother Roger of Taizé. Each of these char-acteristics, in its own way, helps to explain his special kind of sim-plicity as he attempts to understand himself, others and God.

• Spiritual truth is best taught through *parables,* rather than through propositional blueprints for action or belief.

Brother Roger tries his best to avoid telling people they should do this or that. Rather, he sees his life and that of the other brothers as a parable, or story, which illustrates a spiritual truth. "The realities of the Kingdom are especially lived through para-bles," he says.

Sometimes he is so intent on avoiding absolute pronouncements about the spiritual realm that he seems almost evasive: A direct question put to him will often elicit an indirect response.

• As a person's spirituality deepens and his life becomes more of a parable that expresses divine truth, he inevitably becomes more *childlike.*

"God gives us a childlike heart, which he can use to express his truths through living parables rather than words," Brother Roger says. "Of course, words are important—I don't want to be anti-in-tellectual. I have much admiration for scientific research, includ-ing studies that help us find more food in the world, increase our physical resources and provide better medical care. But the child's heart has the simple intuitions which can best communicate spiri-tual values through life, and not through words."

• Brother Roger's inner progress toward this childlike state of spiritual simplicity appears to be one of the key factors that enable him to *relate well to young people.*

He's completely nonjudgmental in his conversations with them. Rather than giving them direct advice, he prefers to assist them in "searching beneath their hearts to find what is hurting deep within themselves. I ask God to have the spirit of discernment. I know that you learn discernment as you practice it; and maybe as you grow older you are quicker in discerning. But you also make many mistakes. There is no man who is infallible."

He says that often when he goes to meetings and sees "those churches full of young people, I think of my own youth. I want only to speak with a child's heart. That way, any shyness I may have with young people disappears. I don't want them to come to see a man: There's nothing more terrible than the vocation of 'public man.' I'm not a public person. I'm like everyone else, with all the same struggles. Every day it's necessary for me to get up in the morning and start the day, just like other people."

His approach to young people has probably been the most successful part of his personal ministry and of the outreach of the Taizé Community. The Taizé brothers have always had a special place in their hearts for young people. But in 1970 Brother Roger announced a more concerted effort to reach out to young men and women in the name of Christ. The vehicle for this new thrust would be a "Council of Youth"—which would bring together young people from all denominations and nations for a variety of meetings and meditations on how spiritual truth can change their lives and the condition of the world at large.

The first meeting, which was held in Taizé in August 1974, involved an estimated forty thousand young people from all over Europe and other parts of the world. They camped in tents on the hillsides around the brothers' community, intensified their personal search for God through contemplation and group discussions, and began to outline ways their lives could make a difference in society.

In the years that followed, other mass gatherings gave impetus for concrete work by young people in poor areas around the world. They were motivated to share both materially and spiritually with those who had less than they did.

In the meantime the "Council of Youth" has been put aside provisionally because people were coming to Taizé in ever greater numbers and Brother Roger did not want the Council to become a "movement" attached to Taizé. He wants young people to come there to search for God, to seek in God a meaning for their lives.

In recognition of Brother Roger's work with young people in Europe, the Templeton Foundation awarded him the 1974 Templeton Prize for Progress in Religion—along with the sum of

£40,000. At the award ceremonies in London, Brother Roger said that the money would go to "poor young people, especially in the southern hemisphere, who, committed in the ways of struggle and contemplation, are seeking to meet one another and to be tireless seekers of communion." In addition, he allotted a sum for the British Isles, "for young people working among immigrants from Africa and Asia, especially Pakistanis, and also for young people struggling for reconciliation in Northern Ireland."

• In his personal spiritual journey, Brother Roger is always willing to take *risks*.

"The pastoral vocation within us does not permit us to remain behind," Brother Roger says. "We have to expose ourselves, confront evil, take risks. God empowers Christian men and women to take risks for others but without using violence."

But at the same time, in extreme cases, he would not rule out the use of violence if it were in order to protect the helpless in a lawless environment. "I would not allow someone in front of me to hurt a child," he explains. "In the history of humanity, there are cases when much courage is necessary to make a tyrant disappear. But I'm not talking about defending oneself; rather, I mean helping helpless women, old people or children.

"There are cases where the law of the jungle is in effect—when all the powers of oppression are given to the one with the most muscular power. I lived in a slum in the southern hemisphere where the police never entered. It was the law of the jungle. If one fails to protect the women and children there, where the strongest person is the law, that can be horrible. I would not have known those situations if I hadn't lived there, and if my brothers didn't now live there. I realized what terrible things can happen in the human community when people close their eyes to suffering and torture."

• The theme of *reconciliation* is also at the center of Brother Roger's thought and life.

"As I grow older, I notice that Christians can achieve reconciliation by being at the heart of the wounds of the human family," he says. "It's when we enter into the divisions of the human family that we realize we can no longer remain separated."

This reconciliation involves, first of all, healing the wounds of division that separate Christian believers—including those from the Protestant and Catholic traditions. "Those involved in ecumenical dialogues often take each other so seriously that they upset each other," he observes. "The Body of Christ is a communion which is much more demanding than simply a group of human beings accepting each other in their differences. Communion is forgiving one another continually. It's loving one another. It's trusting in the gifts that God has placed in someone else. To live in communion in the Church is to participate already in the realities of the Kingdom of God."

But secondly, reconciliation encompasses those outside the Church. "God speaks to all men," Brother Roger says. And as a means of encouraging ties with non-Christians, he believes that Christians should, in humility, recognize that they can learn from nonbelievers.

For example, he points to an old man in Taizé who had gone through bankruptcy as a farmer and who showered the brothers with advice because he wanted to help them avoid his mistakes. "He loved us, even though he had no faith in God."

And then there were some old women in the neighborhood who were unbelievers. "Their blinding generosity astonished us. They were very poor; they didn't have anything. But they still wanted to help us—even though we were used to refusing gifts."

Roger often feels drawn to people like this and is able to ignore religious differences, in part because of what they can show him about God. "With Christians, it's often not love that dominates, but judgments. Frequently, the love of neighbor comes through in people who don't know who God is. Love may arise more spontaneously from them than from certain Christians."

• For Brother Roger, mature spirituality involves *transparency*—especially with those fellow believers who are closest to you.

Transparency means being open and vulnerable with others—having no desire to dissemble or hide from them. To achieve this kind of openness, Brother Roger says, it's sometimes necessary to be "violent with yourself"—a French expression meaning that you have to do some self-examination and give up unnecessary inner reserve and constraints and be willing to trust others more fully.

But even as he advocates this kind of transparency, Brother Roger cautions that "every human being is unique before God. You can't spread your interior—everything that is happening inside —before others. There must be respect for one's identity." In other words, if a person reveals himself indiscriminately to others, that may become emotionally destructive rather than spiritually constructive.

But still, there must always be one or two people to whom you can reveal all, without reservation. "You can't live without speaking of yourself totally with another. And God always gives to us those spiritual mothers and fathers who can understand everything. But that is not spreading one's difficulties before everyone. Always, my whole life, I've had someone like that. One person is enough."

So Brother Roger of Taizé is a man who stands for simple spiritual values—yet his approach to faith and the social action that arises from it are by no means simplistic.

The simplicity he has achieved, both in his outer and inner life, is a quality that has only come about over a period of time, after considerable prayer, thought and practical experience. The childlike perspective on life that he regards as so important hasn't come easily. And by his own admission, he hasn't by any means "arrived" at any state of spiritual perfection.

But at least one thing seems obvious: He has succeeded in creating a kind of parable of simplicity at Taizé which serves as a commentary on those words of Jesus in Matthew 18:3: ". . . unless you turn and become like children, you will never enter the kingdom of heaven."

14

Sarvepalli Radhakrishnan
A Modern-day Philosopher-King

Plato, in his *Republic*, as translated by H. D. P. Lee, describes the ideal political ruler, the "philosopher-king" or "philosopher-ruler," this way:

• He has a "passion for wisdom of every kind without distinction."

• He is "ready to taste every form of knowledge, is glad to learn and never satisfied."

• The philosopher-rulers are those "whose hearts are fixed on Reality itself."

• "He will never willingly tolerate an untruth, but will hate it as much as he loves truth."

• The philosopher "will be self-controlled and not grasping about money."

• He "won't think death anything to be afraid of."

• The philosopher-king will have a "good memory, readiness to learn, breadth of vision and versatility of mind, and be a friend of truth, justice, courage, and discipline."

• Finally, he should also be a person of "education and maturity."

With the relatively low view of politicians that prevails in many Western countries in our own time, many people in reading about this ideal ruler might feel that Plato got caught up in a pipedream.

But he went on to argue, through the words of his teacher, Socrates, that he believed it was quite possible for a philosopher-ruler to take power in a nation under the right circumstances.

Plato, of course, never lived to see the appearance of such a perfect ruler, and it might be argued that no one else has either. But still, there have been some political leaders who at least seem to have come close to his ideal.

In the view of many academic *and* political observers, one such person was the late Sir Sarvepalli Radhakrishnan, the second President of India and the third winner of the Templeton Foundation Prize for Progress in Religion.

Radhakrishnan, who was born in 1888 into a relatively poor family in Tiruttani in Northwest Madras, was educated in Christian missionary schools during his early life. He learned a great deal about Christianity and the New Testament in those formative years, but this education only served to drive him more forcefully back to his Hindu roots.

"My pride as a Hindu, roused by the enterprise and eloquence of Swami Vivekananda, was deeply hurt by the treatment accorded to Hinduism in missionary institutions," he said in *The Radhakrishnan Number*.

So he devoted himself to an intense study of the Vedanta and the philosophy of other world religions. The result was that he eventually formulated an individualistic world view which enabled him to build a kind of intellectual bridge between the East and West as professor of Eastern religions and comparative philosophy at Oxford University. Perhaps even more important, he also had the opportunity to *apply* his world view in the practical arena of Indian politics.

His political involvement began in earnest in 1948 when Prime Minister Jawaharlal Nehru appointed him chairman of an educational commission which was eventually able to exercise decisive influence on the government's education policies. In 1949 his political star continued to rise as he became Indian Ambassador to the Soviet Union.

Then he became Vice President of India in 1962; and finally, he was elected President in 1962 and served two terms, until 1967.

Although the position of President carried more ceremonial

significance than political power, Radhakrishnan made effective use of this platform in influencing governmental policy. And the political stands that he took more often than not reflected his own deeply held personal beliefs about human morality and social ethics. So, to understand the way that Radhakrishnan's thinking influenced his political actions—and why many observers began to compare him to Plato's "philosopher-king"—it will be helpful to examine his personal philosophy of life.

First of all, Radhakrishnan affirmed a universalistic, typically Hindu approach to other religious faiths: He believed that all religions were different ways of pointing toward the same ultimate truth. Still, as is evident in his criticisms of Christianity and other faiths, he felt, as one scholar has said, that Hinduism was "Religion," while other systems of belief were "religions." In other words, Hinduism—and in particular, his interpretation of Hinduism—came closer to pure, unadulterated truth than any other form of belief.

"To claim that any one religious tradition bears unique witness to the truth and reveals the presence of the true God is inconsistent with belief in a living God who has spoken to men 'by diverse portions and in diverse manners,'" he said. (*The Philosophy of Sarvepalli Radhakrishnan*, ed. by Paul A. Schilpp) "If we reflect on the matter deeply we will perceive the unity of spiritual aspiration and endeavour underlying the varied upward paths indicated in the different world faiths. The diversity in the traditional formulations tends to diminish as we climb up the scale of spiritual perfection. All the paths of ascent lead to the mountain top."

Although he said at one point that he was looking for "fellowship" rather than "fusion" of different religions, it's evident from many of his writings that he put tremendous stress on unity among humans of every religious and political persuasion. And this means that eventually he expected that a "universal faith" would appear. At that future time, he said, the old religions "will have to transform themselves into the universal faith or they will fade away."

This firm belief in the necessity of a harmony of religious beliefs had definite implications for Radhakrishnan's political philosophy as well. He said, "Religious idealism seems to be the most hopeful political instrument for peace which the world has ever seen. We cannot reconcile men's conflicting interests and hopes so long as we take our stand on duties and rights. Treaties and diplomatic understandings may restrain passions, but they do not remove fear. The world must be involved with a love of humanity. We want religious heroes who will not wait for the transformation of the whole world but assert with their lives, if necessary, the truth of the conviction, 'On earth one family.' " (S. K. Ray, *The Political Thought of President Radhakrishnan*)

So for Radhakrishnan, a personal belief in the unity of all peoples, and in the importance of expressing love to others, extended naturally to the broader social and political scene. Or as he put it, "The things of Caesar should be related to the things of God. Spiritual values must permeate the world of life. Religion is not an opiate for the disorders of the spirit. It is a dynamic for social advance. Unless we have faith in an inner order, we cannot build a stable outer order."

Specifically, he wanted to see a progression of society from the law of the jungle; to the rule of law; to the highest political level, where nonviolence and unselfishness prevailed. With respect to his belief in the possibility of this highest level of social and political reality, he owed a great deal to the influence of Mahatma Gandhi's philosophy of nonviolence.

So Radhakrishnan had a belief system that made him a candidate for a "philosopher-king" in the style of Plato's ideal. And in 1962 he got the opportunity of a lifetime to realize that goal when he was elected President of India.

He wasted no time speaking out strongly for the implementation of his beliefs after he took office. In a 1963 Independence Day broadcast to the Indian nation, for instance, he lauded recent developments on a nuclear test ban agreement between the United States and the Soviet Union, and also plans for mutual cooperation between those two countries for exploration of outer space. Both he and Nehru had been pleading for those agreements and also for peaceful settlements of various international disputes.

But soon the problem of trying to settle international quarrels came much closer to home. In 1965 Prince Ayub Khan announced that his nation, Pakistan, was at war with India. But Radhakrishnan, always reacting consistently with his personal philosophy, responded: "We in India do not regard ourselves as at war with Pakistan; we have friendly feelings for the people of Pakistan and have been careful to do precisely no more than what is required to safeguard our territorial integrity and Federated Union which includes Jammu and Kashmir."

But at the same time, he wasn't living in some ivory tower during the conflict with Pakistan. He was quick to congratulate the Indian officers and soldiers on their courage, heroism and sacrifice, and he took a firm position against what he regarded as Pakistan's acts of aggression.

But despite these concessions to patriotism, the posture he wanted India to assume was purely a defensive one. In other words, he said, "This conflict has been forced on us because there has been a persistent and continuous attempt, since August 5 [1965], by Pakistan to take the law into its own hands and to upset by force the legitimately established government in the State of Jammu and Kashmir.

"But in the midst of this tragic conflict thrust on us by our neighbor, I wish to remind you that we should not and cannot forget our traditions, our ideals and our history. We detest war and all its horrors. Our troops have so far only fought for peace and for the defense of our land."

And Radhakrishnan wanted to keep it that way—a defense-oriented war on the part of India. Of course, the tendency in the general population and among many Indian political leaders was to get aggressively nationalistic in such a military crisis.

But he responded in quite a different way from what you would expect from the average government leader. For example, he cautioned his people in one speech: "We have been adopting for centuries the retaliatory attitude of life—wickedness for the wicked. But Gandhi displaced this attitude with that of love even for the enemy. Are we doing it?"

These are by no means typical words from a typical politician. But then, Radhakrishnan wasn't, by any definition, very typical. Even as he advocated the importance of unity of all human beings, he backed up his words with support of practical programs that gave the poor of India the right to have food distributed to them if they needed it.

In 1963 he broadcast this stern message to the nation: "A recent report shows that food adulteration is being practiced on a large scale. Of all antisocial practices there is none more heinous than adulteration of foodstuffs. The practitioners of this evil, the hoarders, the profiteers, the black-marketeers and the speculators, are among the worst enemies of our society. They have to be dealt with sternly, however well-placed, important or influential they may be."

So in addition to being a thoroughgoing peace advocate on the international scene, Radhakrishnan was a crusader for the rights of the "little man" and a committed enemy of corruption in high places at home.

It's interesting to speculate on what he might have done—or what consternation he might have caused among professional politicians and bureaucrats—if he had been able to wield any real power. Such a "philosopher-king" as Prime Minister in India, rather than President, would have been Plato's dream.

But even though the Indian presidency did not carry the power of coercion, it did carry the power of reason, as one of his political colleagues noted later. And this moral authority may, in the long run, have given a man like Radhakrishnan more influence than if he had actually been able to wage war and peace.

He was—and remains, even after his death in 1975—a symbol of high, pure values in the pragmatic and sometimes unprincipled world of daily politics. So whether one agrees or not with his philosophical orientation, Radhakrishnan's life must stand as an example for all who would test the authenticity of their beliefs in the hostile atmosphere of the practical world.

15

Cardinal Suenens
Pioneer of the
Charismatic Renewal

Real religion only has true meaning and the capacity to change lives when it possesses power—a supernatural kind of power. In Christianity that power is synonymous with the Spirit of God.

Jesus, for example, just before his ascension, said: ". . . you shall receive power when the Holy Spirit has come upon you. . . ." (Acts 1:8) And the story of Christ's followers in establishing the early church is the story of healings, conversions and miracles, all accomplished through the power of the Spirit.

Periodically throughout Christian history the power of the Spirit has manifested itself through unusual spiritual phenomena and forces. And in our own day there is evidence that the Spirit is working again in marvelous and beneficial ways—especially in the Charismatic Movement which has swept through most major denominations and communions and is providing an exciting new basis for Christian unity.

The Charismatic Movement derives its name from the Greek root *charisma*, which means "gift" or, in the New Testament context, spiritual gifts. The Scriptural authority for this gift concept is 1 Corinthians 12–14, where St. Paul describes various gifts of the Spirit, such as healing, speaking in tongues (glossolalia), miracles and prophecy. Modern charismatics believe that the gifts listed in the New Testament church are as valid and available today as they were in the first century: The believer only needs to ask for those powers and believe God will grant them in order to receive them.

The Charismatic Movement, which has been a strong force for renewal since about 1960, is related to the modern Pentecostal Movement, which arose in the early twentieth century and engendered several new denominations.

But the difference is that the Charismatic Movement has remained just that—a movement. Those who identify with the charismatic way of thinking and believing have chosen to remain in their original denominations and often have become catalysts for spiritual renewal there. The millions of Christians who identify with the Charismatic Movement believe that they are experiencing many of the New Testament gifts.

In some quarters of church leadership there is considerable nervousness about this unpredictable new expression of the power of the Spirit because it's a phenomenon that's difficult to control. You can't institutionalize the "blowing" of the Spirit: Or as Jesus said, the Spirit is as impossible to contain as the wind: "The wind blows where it wills, and you hear the sound of it, but you do not know whence it comes or whither it goes; so it is with every one who is born of the Spirit." (John 3:8)

So this sort of spiritual exuberance, with its potential for radical individuality, can be threatening to the established church; and, in fact, it may actually do harm—for example, by causing divisiveness in local congregations if the wrong leaders are in charge. As a result, one of the great needs of the Charismatic Movement has been responsible leadership to direct this powerful force toward church renewal, rather than ecclesiastical chaos.

God has raised a number of such leaders, and one of the most influential has been Leon Joseph Cardinal Suenens, Archbishop of Malines-Brussels and Primate of Belgium.

As the highest-ranking Roman Catholic among the charismatics, Cardinal Suenens has been generally regarded as one of the movement's most influential and helpful leaders. Since his own intense experience with the Spirit in 1973, he has become increasingly aware of the great potential of the Charismatic Movement as a unifying force between Christians and non-Christians alike. In particular, he has discovered the major role the movement can play in bringing an individual into a closer personal relationship with God; in drawing members of a family closer together; and in providing a basis for the broad ecumenical movement, which seeks to find institutional ways to bind various Christian groups together.

But Cardinal Suenens' decisive experiences with the Spirit of God did not occur until he was well along in his religious career. Born in 1904, he was educated by priests in Belgium before going to Rome for further training at age seventeen.

At twenty-three he was ordained as a priest, and he continued his studies in Rome to receive doctorates in philosophy and theology. Suenens was eventually appointed professor of philosophy at the seminary at Malines in Belgium, and when World War II ended, he became Auxiliary Bishop to Cardinal van Roey. Upon the cardinal's death, Suenens was named Archbishop of Malines. He became a cardinal in 1962.

Throughout his career as a priest, he was attracted by the Holy Spirit. And, in fact, he chose the motto "In the Holy Spirit" when he became a bishop in 1945.

But his first profound personal experience with the Spirit didn't come until 1948. "I first felt the presence of the Lord very deeply," he said of that encounter. "It was my first experience, my first baptism. I strongly felt the love of God in a personal way, that He was asking me to do His will. I felt the Spirit of God blowing through me. I felt at the time, 'I cannot direct the wind, but I can adjust my sails.' "

But that initial encounter with the Spirit's power was just a beginning. In an interview at the International Eucharistic Congress in Philadelphia in 1976, he explained his later experiences with the Spirit this way: "I believe that everybody is converted five times or more. And I discovered the Holy Spirit more and more, until one day in 1973 I encountered the charismatic renewal in the United States. For me, that was an important moment. It was not a peak experience, but rather a release of the Spirit [in me]. I gained the courage to speak more freely about the Spirit, to let Him speak in me and make me more instrumental."

Cardinal Suenens says that during that 1973 experience he "asked a few friends of mine to pray for me in that same Spirit, as they do in the charismatic renewal, kneeling down and asking. I didn't feel anything special the day after. But after a certain time,

I felt I was becoming freer and freer. It was a feeling of not being afraid to show your faith, not being afraid to express it strongly—without inhibitions."

For Cardinal Suenens, speaking in tongues, healing experiences and other "gifts of the Spirit" followed. But perhaps his most enduring contributions after this encounter with the Spirit have been in promoting greater unity among Christian believers of all persuasions.

For example, he has attended many meetings and discussions with Anglicans and Episcopalians, in an effort to overcome ecclesiastical differences through a grass-roots unity in God's Spirit. In his book *A New Pentecost* he describes how he and Dr. Michael Ramsey, the former Archbishop of Canterbury, sat down for a heart-to-heart talk in Malines. Cardinal Suenens suggested that they open the New Testament to "ask a word of the Lord." And the verse that first caught their eye was John 20:26: "Despite the locked doors, Jesus came and stood before them. 'Peace be with you,' he said."

The cardinal interpreted this "word" as indicating that even though the doors were still closed between Anglicans and Catholics, Jesus was in the midst of them saying, "Peace be with you." And the time of unity was nearer than many might think.

But even as he works diligently toward greater unity among Christians, Cardinal Suenens refuses to compromise what he regards as the fundamental truth of the Gospel for the sake of fellowship. "I cannot have Christian dialogue with Christians who do not believe in the Resurrection or in the Pentecost," he says. "True Christians believe that the Father sent His only Son on earth to redeem us, to become our Savior. We will find resurrection through Him and be reborn in Him. We will see in Him the promise of the Father: I will send you my Spirit forever and ever. That's the key of my faith."

But with this firm commitment to sound doctrine as the "bottom line" in his faith, he still opens his arms wide to welcome complete fellowship with any true Christian believer, from any social or ecclesiastical level or tradition. "It is often thought that the charismatic gifts are only for holy people, for those in monasteries —holy monks somewhere," he says. "But that's not so. They were promised by God for those who receive the Spirit. Even just for a moment somebody can be inspired to say just the words you wish to hear, because the Lord wishes it to be said by somebody."

This open attitude by Cardinal Suenens toward the working of the Spirit once even drew in Pope John Paul II. "Once I celebrated Mass with the Holy Father in his private chapel," the cardinal recalls. "I said to the charismatics with me, 'Pray in tongues during the time of Holy Communion. Just go ahead.' So they sang in tongues and prayed a moment in tongues. After the Mass, I said, 'Holy Father, did we disturb you with our praying in tongues?' And he said, 'Oh, no. It helped me to pray more deeply!'"

So from Pope to lay parishioner, from Protestant to Catholic to Orthodox, Cardinal Suenens believes that the Spirit is at work—and he actively encourages and promotes that work.

And there's still more, a still broader belief he has about the Spirit. Even though he is adamant about the importance of historic Christian doctrine, he still believes that "where something is right and true and honest and peaceful—the Spirit is there. That's the sign of the presence of the Spirit. Even if a man doesn't know the name, the Spirit is in all religions of the world. Wherever people are following their consciences honestly, doing the best they can, being nice and practicing love—the Holy Spirit is there."

He's encountered this far-ranging work of the Spirit in his own experiences with non-Christians too. For example, he recalls one friend of his who is an agnostic and a publisher of a political review. This man, though he has no faith, revealed to Cardinal Suenens that he believed in original sin—though he expressed it in quite different terms from the usual theological statements.

Among other things, this agnostic said: "I don't believe in original sin, but if you don't accept it, you are stupid. Every day I see it with my eyes. People are not naturally just good. They are both good and weak."

It was the very newness and freshness of the man's description that gave the cardinal further insights into his own long-held beliefs.

Even as Cardinal Suenens observes the Spirit working in such diverse ways and places, he is careful to be certain that the Spirit remains in power in his own life. And there are at least two major ways he nurtures his own spiritual strength.

First of all, he maintains a sensitivity to the Spirit through private prayer. "Everyone has his own way to pray," he explains. "Mine is to walk and talk conversationally with the Lord. For me, walking with the Lord is the easiest way to be alive and to listen to Him. I will then open my missal up every day and see the message of the Lord for me for that day. You must allow yourself a time of freedom, a time for praying in your daily life. Even though the circumstances are so strong that you are always busy, you *must* keep an oasis of peace and prayer and just be with the Lord."

Secondly, he maintains the presence of the Spirit through his regular association with "a group of friends whom I have known for a long time. They are not priests, but lay people. When we are together, I am on the same level as they are. I am not chief in any way. So we can share fully and be very open. Every Christian in the world needs brothers and sisters—a little community around him. To keep your faith alive, you have to be supported in a group."

So Cardinal Suenens is a man of action, a man with a mission, who finds his strength through a very profound relationship with the Spirit of God. He is always on the go, always ready to support any authentic efforts to bring about unity between Christians and understandings among all peoples.

Also, in a very real sense, his ultimate goal is to do away with the very movement, the Charismatic Movement, in which he is so deeply involved. "It is my impossible dream to Christianize Christians," he says. "We must show visibly a community of the Spirit— a unity among the main churches. My life is consecrated to the charismatic renewal—particularly to the ecumenical dimension of it.

"But there should not be a [charismatic] church next to a [traditional] church. The movement should be a renewal of the entire church and should disappear into it. For the same reason, the ecumenical movement will some day disappear because we will all become one."

For his profound insights into the workings of God's Spirit and his hard work on behalf of greater understanding between those of widely divergent beliefs, Cardinal Suenens was awarded the Templeton Prize for Progress in Religion in 1976. But it is

Suenens' belief that progress toward the full work of God's Spirit has only just begun.

The Charismatic Movement, he concludes, is like springtime. "Spring is giving new life to the trees, to the flowers, to the birds, to the skies, touching everything. Everywhere the Spirit is, it makes everything alive—putting strength in your body, your fingers, your feet, and your heart."

16

Chiara Lubich
Founder of the
Focolare Movement

There are always a few individuals who somehow seem able to change things for the better. They rarely "toot their own horns," and often we're not even aware they're around—at least, not until they're absent.

Jesus called these special people "the salt of the earth" and "the light of the world." Most people like being around these individuals because they have the ability to turn the negative into the positive. They also know how to pep things up and encourage others to count their blessings rather than their shortcomings. And they know something about how to point others beyond human goodness to the source of that goodness.

Jesus seemed to know there would never be great crowds of these upbeat, vital people. But He also suggested that, despite their limited numbers, they would always make a big difference, wherever they were found.

In many ways, then, these special agents of God are in an enviable position. They know exactly who they are and what they are intended to do in life. They have no need for public acclaim or affirmation for their good works, because their motivation to live a certain way comes from within, not from without. And since they are so secure inside, they usually remain relaxed and joyous, even as they confront the inevitable pressures and frustrations of life.

What does it take to become such a self-assured, spiritually sensitive person?

To answer this question, let's take a few lessons from a motherly, sixtyish Italian woman by the name of Chiara Lubich, the founder and guiding light behind the Roman Catholic Focolare Movement.

Chiara was born Silvia Lubich in Trent, Italy, in 1920. It was years later, at the time she came to understand her vocation, or main purpose in life, that she changed her name to "Chiara," in honor of St. Clare of Assisi, the most prominent female follower of St. Francis of Assisi.

Chiara's family were Catholics, business people who had fallen upon hard times as a result of the general economic deterioration of the nation. So she grew up in an environment which offered plenty of spiritual nurturance, but little of the material things of life.

Like many people who came from such humble family origins, Chiara was an achiever. She was a good student and wanted to study philosophy. But because of the war she had to alter her plans, so at the age of eighteen she became an instructor in a one-room schoolhouse in a northern Italian village near Trent.

Despite her commitment to a teaching career, however, Chiara's life was by no means a settled and immutable thing in those days. She was at an important age, the late teen-age years, which marks one of those watersheds in our lives—perhaps similar to the so-called "midlife crisis" experienced by those in their late thirties and forties. These are times when many people become more sensitive to the spiritual and psychological forces around and inside them.

To explain what often happens inside young people on the threshold of adulthood, psychologist Erik H. Erikson, in his *Young Man Luther* and other works, introduced the now well-known concept of the "identity crisis." He pinpointed the late teens and early twenties as "an age which can be most painfully aware of the need for decisions, most driven to choose new devotions and to discard old ones. . . ."

To put all this in more spiritual terms, you might say there are certain ages when many people are especially open to God's dramatic intervention in their lives. This sort of revelation may be characterized as a conversion, renewal or other deep insight or commitment which is part of a divine lifetime plan for the individual.

Of course, the overwhelming power of a genuine revelation from God—and not mere psychology—is the key to this sort of experience, just as it was for St. Paul when he encountered Jesus in the blinding light on the road to Damascus. According to the biblical account, it was certainly God's will more than Paul's readiness that brought about this conversion. But still, there is some reason to think that most men and women tend to be more open to God's presence and word at certain sensitive times in their lives, and it's at these times that He frequently chooses to move in and make Himself known.

As for Chiara Lubich, she was certainly ready in her late teens and early twenties for God to act decisively in her life. And act, He did!

In 1939, when she was nineteen, Chiara traveled to a Catholic student convention in the Italian town of Loreto. As she tells the story, it was the most important trip of her life up to that time. When she arrived in Loreto she immediately visited the little house-shrine which is "like a pearl set within a great fortified church. Tradition says that this house is the house of the family of Nazareth, and that the angels moved it from place to place, finally leaving it [in Loreto]."

Upon entering that little house, Chiara was deeply moved, as the open windows in her own soul freely admitted the exhilarating winds of the Spirit of God. "I was thinking of Mary, Jesus, Joseph, and I could imagine them going from one place to the other in the house. I thought that through the window, which is in the rear of the house, perhaps the angel had announced the Incarnation to Mary. And I was thinking that perhaps those walls had resounded with the singing of Mary and the voice of Jesus.

"As I was leaning against those walls, blackened from time, it seemed that the supernatural was almost overpowering me. And I was crying. This happened every day, because every day I would go into that extraordinary place, and I would remain there, immersed in the same contemplation."

So she wept almost continuously as she visited that shrine day after day. Finally, on the last day, her encounter with the Spirit reached a culmination. The church was filled with many young women wearing white veils, and Chiara recalls, "I had the impression that many, many would follow me in virginity. I went back to Trent with the conviction that I had found my way in life. It was not the way of a natural family; nor the way of a convent. Neither was it only to live a celibate life, [while] remaining in the world. It was something which had the beauty of these three vocations."

For Chiara, then, what God had shown her was a fourth way—which later came to be known as the *focolare,* or "fireside" movement. The name suggests a community of individuals who live in the same house or apartment—or at least have a strong family-like orientation—and are bound together by commitments to God and to each other.

But at the time of her Loreto experience, nineteen-year-old Chiara had no idea exactly what form this "fourth way" would take. So she continued her work as a teacher during the next few years, and she also kept listening for the voice of God.

Then, paradoxically, as Italian lives, towns and regions were being shattered and torn asunder in 1943 at the height of the destruction and chaos of the Second World War, everything began to come together for Chiara. She was working at the time as a private instructor because regular classroom studies had been suspended as a result of the war. It was during this period that she realized she had been given a special gift from God—or, to use the New Testament Greek word, a *charisma.*

As to exactly when and how this realization came upon her, she says, "I couldn't tell you the exact moment, but I was teaching philosophy to a young woman who became one of my first companions. One day, I was telling her about the theories of Kant. I was very taken by these ideas, and therefore I was 'dragging' my friend with me.

"Then, all of a sudden, a thought came to me: 'How far this trend of thought is from the truth of the resurrection of the flesh!' "

Hanging above her desk was a picture of Jesus, and Chiara, obeying an inexorable inner impulse, reached over to touch the painting. "I put my hand on His heart, and I said, 'I believe in the resurrection of the flesh, even if I do not see.' In fact, in order to affirm with greater strength my faith, I remember saying, 'I *swear* that I believe in the resurrection of the flesh!' "

In other words, a great transformation was taking place inside Chiara, who began to call herself "Chiara"—or "Clare"—instead of "Silvia" during this period. As brilliant a young woman as she was, she became impressed in the most profound way that intellect was not enough. For her to be able to live a joyously consistent Christian life and to be able to help others establish a relationship with God, she realized that her commitment to Christ had to reach down to the very depths of the heart, to the roots of the human will and the wellsprings of personal identity.

At Loreto, four years before, God had grasped her and started preparing her for a great work. Now He was completing that revelation and communicating to her what that work would be. An inner process of spiritual progress was occurring inside her which was strengthening her and preparing her to work for a broader kind of spiritual progress in the world at large.

"In that moment, it was as if my mind opened up," she recalls. "I don't remember a word of what I said then [to my female companion], but I remember that the truth of our faith was as evident to me in that moment as the theories of Kant. I understood then, as I understood later in other moments, that there is a light which comes from above. It is a light which is not a fruit of our intelligence, but which comes from God."

This "light from above," which originates not in our minds but in our Maker and emits its warm, enlightening glow from the very center of our beings, became the key to her later work. From this point on, she devoted her life to making her thoughts and her actions one: Her "ideal" in life, as she called it, became the establishment of concentric circles of unity and love, beginning with herself and moving outward to her close companions, to other brothers and sisters in her faith, and finally to the world at large.

This path Chiara had chosen involved living the Gospel literally and radically in the pressure-packed world around her—the very world that was now being ravaged by a terrible global war. But her life and work were to be measured only by the standards of God which were written on the heart, not by the world around her. So from the very beginning, she and her few companions operated quietly and privately.

Those whose lives they touched and whose needs they met were acutely aware of their unselfish devotion and love. But it was almost as though they were saying to others, as Jesus had said to both the leper and the blind man, "Take care that no one learns about this." (Matthew 9:30; cf. Matthew 8:4) For as powerful as it was, their good work remained largely unknown to the public.

On December 7, 1943, Chiara had made vows to God that her life would always be devoted to him—just as a faithful bride makes a permanent commitment to her husband-to-be. Now Chiara's future was irrevocably in God's hands. Among other things, this commitment came to mean living a celibate life in the company of other women who affirmed the same need to offer a quiet but powerful Christian witness in secular society.

Chiara took the first steps in putting her spiritual vision into practice as she and a small group of friends began to meet together to pray, read the Bible, and serve the poor in the war-torn city of Trent. But if these young women, who ranged in age from fifteen to twenty-five, had possessed anything less than a total commitment to Christ, they would have quickly fallen by the wayside.

The bombings got worse, and Chiara and her family at one point decided to flee the city to escape one particularly devastating air raid. As they looked back on Trent from the hills that overlooked the city, they could see houses exploding and collapsing as death-dealing bombs descended from the airplanes.

Chiara's family decided to move away to escape the terror, and that presented her with a wrenching decision between her dearest loved ones and her divinely ordained vocation. Most of the young women in her new spiritual community suffered even greater personal losses, such as the destruction of homes and the death of loved ones. But one by one they gathered together in Trent and decided to stay there to build their community and serve the poor. And even though Chiara's relatives had left, she remained to assume leadership of the work of her spiritual sisters.

It was at this time that those who observed the courageous work of these young people began to call them the *focolare* community. They were bound together as a close-knit family might be at the hearth or fireside of a home—even though they didn't have any real home at first, but only a series of dark, damp air-raid shelters. Also, the name was appropriate because of the flame of faith that motivated them and the love for others and for God that glowed in their hearts. The "focolarini" radiate love as a fireside radiates heat.

So they met in those Italian air-raid shelters as many as eleven times a day, praying and deepening their relationship with one another as planes bombed the village about them. And they constantly sought concrete answers to the question, "What is the Ideal—the truly Christ-centered way of life—which is worth following and which no bomb can destroy?" And as they asked and searched, the answers gradually came.

For example, Chiara says they learned the incredibly profound, life-changing dimensions of simple, easily overlooked biblical terms, like the word "as" in the Gospels: "love your neighbor *as* yourself"; "love one another *as* I have loved you"; "*as* the Father has sent me. . . ." She explains this particular insight this way: "God really wants us to love our neighbor *as*—and that means in the same, identical way that we love ourselves. We understood this at that time and tried to put it into practice."

From the beginning—even in those early days while these few young women huddled together and read the Gospel in scary, uncomfortable bomb shelters, two words emerged as slogans to guide their lives—*love* and *unity*.

As for love, one verse that kept coming back in their conversations and echoing in their minds was Jesus' words in John 13:34: ". . . love one another; just as I have loved you, you also must love one another."

Chiara came to believe that the major mark of spiritual maturity is "one's love of neighbor. You can see how much a person loves God from how much he loves his neighbor. Also, love of neighbor is that which helps us to become mature. In fact, the love of neighbor makes the love of God in us grow."

This powerful love which emanates from God and moves out to conquer the world through the thoroughly committed Christian led quite naturally to Chiara's conviction that the most important distinction of human social interaction should involve a special kind of unity or oneness.

"The deeper the root of a little plant is into the earth, the more the plant grows and goes up toward the sky," she said. "So, for Christians, the more they make themselves one with others, the more they love others, the more the love of God grows in [the individual Christian] as well.

"This was an experience of ours from the beginning. The Lord was urging us very forcefully to love our neighbor, to love Jesus in him. And we would try to live like that all day long, to make ourselves one with all the persons we met, to share their joys and their sufferings, and to make ourselves one with their aspirations. In doing that, we would notice in the evenings, when we recollected ourselves in prayer, that we had found a certain union with God, even if we were at the beginning of our spiritual life."

Jesus had prayed in His "high priestly prayer" in John 17:21: "May they all be one. Father, may they be one in us, as you are in me and I in you, so that the world may believe it was you who sent me." And Chiara and her companions set out to make this prayer of Christ a reality.

She explains further: "The Gospel has to do with unity in a particular way. Today in the world, we witness many divisions. For instance, in families we see divorces and separations between husband and wife. There are also other divisions among members of the same family—gaps among generations, walls between children, parents and the elderly.

"There exists great intolerance among people living in the same environment. In the same nation, there are divisions among opposing parties and different factions. There are wars. Racism is still alive.

"If we look at Christianity as a whole we see the wound of disunity among the churches. There are struggles among people of different confessions, as is now seen in Northern Ireland.

"At this moment in history, it is necessary to *underline* unity."

The dynamic element that takes Chiara's convictions about love and unity out of the realm of abstract ideas and ordinary expressions of piety, and transforms them into something dramatically new—is the fact that she decided, back there in World War II, to *live* her beliefs in the humblest, most personal way. She decided to share her gift, or *charisma*, first with those who were closest to her, those whom God put in her immediate path.

For Chiara, in 1943 and 1944, this meant deepening her love relationships with her closest companions and with the war victims in Trent who first came to her attention. And she resolved to let her work bring joy and satisfaction for its own sake, and not to expect any favorable publicity or human affirmation.

In other words, even though she probably wouldn't put it in these terms, she decided to become humble—to devote herself to a radical and powerful, but low-profile, expression of her faith. Finally, and perhaps most importantly, she *stuck by this decision* year after year.

Everyone knows of examples of "flash-in-the-pan" piety— dramatic conversion or renewal experiences that cause a person to flare up brightly in his church or community. But then, because of some inner deficiency, the ardor of commitment burns out. Also, there are plenty of examples of "lukewarm" faith—the level of commitment that is genuine, but not sufficiently searing to bring about major transformations in a person's way of life.

The faith of Chiara, in contrast, flared up and continued to burn hotly and brightly. As a result, little by little, she gradually grew into the role of an international spiritual leader. As her inner life deepened, she reached out more and more to share her special gift for promoting love and unity among ordinary, "grass-roots" people in every society.

The wide range of her spiritual influence is astounding when you consider what has happened during the forty years since the first "fireside" community got started in Italy. Here are a few highlights:

• In 1948, the first men's *focolare* started, and in the same year, Igino Giordani became the first married *focolarino*.

• Between 1950 and 1958, *focolare* centers opened in major Italian cities, as well as in Germany, Belgium and France.

• In about 1960, Chiara and other *focolare* leaders met with German Lutheran evangelicals and began to take steps to heal the Protestant-Catholic breach which had begun with Martin Luther centuries before.

As Chiara describes one of these meetings: "It was particularly successful because of a special grace and a tremendous joy that filled everyone. Three Anglican persons who happened to be present were also deeply struck."

According to Chiara, the Anglicans reacted to the ecumenical developments this way: "They decided, 'If the Catholics are accomplishing such a deep unity with the Lutherans, they [the

Catholics] will be able to have an even deeper unity with Anglicans, with whom they have greater bonds.' And so they said, 'Now, we want to come with *other* Anglicans. . . .' This is exactly what happened.

"In this way, the Movement developed among the Anglicans in England. Now it is in full bloom: We know that there are about ten thousand Anglicans who are part of the Movement, and several Anglican bishops who are close to the Movement."

• In 1962, the Holy See gave official papal approval to the Focolare Movement. In the years immediately preceding and following this official approval, Chiara and her followers reached out and drew in followers in South America.

• In 1967, Athenagoras I, the Ecumenical Patriarch of Constantinople and leader of the Eastern Orthodox Church, received Chiara in a formal audience. As a result, they became close friends.

Chiara describes the ecumenical implications of their intimate relationship like this: "Patriarch Athenagoras was the one who revealed to us the beauty of the Orthodox Church. I had a deep rapport with him. Also, I knew Pope Paul VI very well; I had known him since 1951 or 1952. So I happened to become a means for the Patriarch to communicate with the Pope—in an unofficial way.

"The Patriarch had this great aspiration: to reestablish, after a thousand years, unity with the Catholic Church. Often I would convey his sentiments, his aspirations, and his desires to Pope Paul. This contributed to the cementing of the unity between these two personalities of the Church. Patriarch Athenagoras was ready to do anything in order to reach 'the one chalice.' On the other hand, Pope Paul VI had an opportunity to develop a tremendous esteem for Patriarch Athenagoras, so much so that when Patriarch Athenagoras died, Paul VI said, 'A saint has died.' "

Chiara had known the Patriarch for about seven years.

In 1977, Chiara Lubich became the fifth winner of the international Templeton Progress in Religion Prize. Upon receiving the check for fifty thousand pounds sterling (then the equivalent of eighty-five thousand dollars), she announced that the money would be used to help alleviate several particularly acute areas of human need.

Part of the prize went to enlarge the maternity wing of a hospital in the little town of Fontem in Cameroons, Africa. Another segment of the award was devoted to building two houses for those who lived in a shantytown in Recife, Brazil. A third portion was used to build the last stage of a religious and social training center for Asians, including residents of Tagaytay in the Philippines. Finally, Chiara decided to keep a part of the prize in Italy for the "Town of Charity" which the diocese of Rome was planning to set up for handicapped people.

From the nineteen-sixties to the present, then, the Focolare Movement has spread throughout the world, with groups in the United States, the Philippines, Australia, Korea and Japan. Married people, who maintain their own homes, and also those who have chosen a celibate life, participate in the *focolare* communities, both to build up their personal faith and to strengthen their community spiritual ties.

Also, through the work of the "Volunteers" (men and women who meet weekly and are especially action-oriented in expressing their faith) and the "Gen" (the children and young people), the Movement has become a service organization on a global scale. *Focolare* sympathizers and followers have built hospitals and cleared swamps in every corner of the world.

But as far-flung as the *focolare* may now be, their fundamental, original purpose of applying Christian unity and love in ordinary personal relationships remains a guiding principle. The quiet, intimate spiritual approach begun during those bombing raids in World War II, where a small group of young women discovered the extraordinary presence of God in their ordinary surroundings, continues to set the tone and establish the spiritual style of the millions who identify with the Movement today.

So if you expect to see the work of the Focolare Movement—or Chiara Lubich—plastered in headlines across the front page of your daily newspaper, you're likely to be disappointed. In fact, unless you happen to be part of the Movement, it's likely that you've never even heard of it, despite the million or more who identify with some phase of their work.

You see, despite Chiara's many speeches and other public appearances, the Focolare Movement is about as low-profile as it's possible for a successful, life-changing spiritual movement to be in

our news-oriented society. In a sense, it really is a spiritual renewal movement, which operates behind the lines of our society's
corruption, insensitivity and moral inconsistency.

All of those connected with the Focolare Movement are involved in one way or another with the mundane world as employees of ordinary companies or members of secular societies
and organizations. So, in that sense, they may be all but invisible
to the casual observer. But to the people who are in contact with
them every day, they are likely to be a breath of fresh air in a
stuffy office, or a tangy, energizing flavor in an otherwise flat,
tasteless environment.

The key thing about the most effective *focolare* followers is
that they have caught a part of Chiara Lubich's original fire, which
began to burn at those spiritual "firesides" in the bomb shelters of
Trent and has now spread to the farthest reaches of the earth. So
even though they don't promote themselves and tend to look to
God rather than man for approval, it's inevitable that the inner
glow that emanates from them will be felt and seen by society at
large.

The main lesson from Chiara and her Focolare Movement,
then, is essentially the same as Jesus' double-edged message in the
Sermon on the Mount: It's important not to practice your piety
before men and, in effect, sound a fanfare each time you go to
worship or perform some good deed. But at the same time, it's essential not to hide the light of your faith under a bushel, so that no
one knows the direction from whence it came.

Or to put all this another way, if you want to be effective spiritually, you must never forget: "You are the light of the world.
. . . your light must shine in the sight of men, so that, seeing your good works, they may give the praise to your Father in
heaven." (Matthew 5:14, 16)

17

Thomas F. Torrance
Guiding Light of the
New Theology of Science

Spending an evening in a lengthy, face-to-face conversation about theology and science with Professor Thomas Torrance is similar to boarding a futuristic spaceship and exploring strange new worlds and universes.

At first, you can't quite focus in on the new concepts and experiences you're encountering. But then gradually the complexity recedes, and a beautiful, inspiring simplicity of thought emerges—a simplicity that convinces you that it's indeed possible, at some point in the ethereal reaches of space and time, for religion and science to merge into a beautiful whole.

Professor Torrance, a former Moderator of the Church of Scotland and former Professor of Christian Dogmatics at the University of Edinburgh, is widely respected among both theologians and scientists for his work on the relationship between science and religion. And it was for his advancement of thought in this area that he was awarded the 1978 Templeton Progress in Religion Prize. John Templeton has said, "I can think of no one who deserves the name of 'genius' more than Torrance."

But it's one thing to hear a brief accolade or read a short newspaper account of who he is and what he's done, and quite another to spend a few hours voyaging into the farthest oceans of his fertile mind. So now let's spend a few pages distilling some of his most stimulating thoughts from one of those lengthy living-room discussions.

A typical Torrance discourse on what is *really* real in the universe ranges over such formidable topics as Einstein's theory of relativity, wave theory, quantum mechanics, and Newtonian physics—not to mention the thoughts of St. Augustine, Barth, Tillich and a host of other theological sages. The Scottish professor is clearly well versed in a stupendous range of interdisciplinary subjects. You might say he possesses a classic seminal mind.

But his academic expertise is not really the essence of his inspiration. For he is not only a scholar; he's also a *believer*—a man who takes a stand on what he knows, unequivocally, to be true about the nature of the universe and the human role in it. All of his vast knowledge is integrated into a powerful unity by the overriding principle of his faith, and that makes his intellectual power even more overwhelming.

For Thomas Torrance, all of history—indeed, all of the universe—revolves around the Incarnation of Jesus Christ. Or as he puts it, "Whatever comes will be bound up with Jesus Christ. From this central point of reference, the whole future will pivot. So the Incarnation, so to speak, is like an axis God has thrust through the universe, and the whole universe revolves around this axis. It's a staggering thought, you know."

In several of his books, including *Space, Time and Incarnation* and *Space, Time and Ressurrection,* he has developed these themes at length. (His other books, which expand still further upon his thought, include *Theological Science, God and Rationality, The Ground and Grammar of Theology,* and *Divine and Contingent Order.*) Because of the Christian assumption he makes about the nature of reality, all of his theoretical speculation is peppered with references to possible relationships between scientific and theological truths.

For example, one line of thought he pursued in one recent informal discussion concerned the nature of light. He began by noting that the book of Genesis says that the first thing to be created was light. "Well, that's also what we know in science," he says. "All bodies in motion are defined in terms of space and time; and space and time are defined in terms of light. Light's the fastest messenger of the universe. I mean, everything we know is finally determined by light, you see. And that concept you already have in the Old Testament in Genesis."

He hastens to add, however, that Genesis "is not giving us a scientific account. Genesis is telling us from God's point of view how to understand the creation."

Now, at this point of the discussion it's important for the neophyte in matters of space, time and theology to step back for a moment and try to think about reality from God's timeless perspective—not from our human orientation of chronological time, where one year follows the next in a nice, orderly progression.

"I think of it this way," Torrance explains. "The last book of the Bible is what we call the Apocalypse. The apocalyptic view is a way of understanding history and future events from the side of God, and God always takes us by surprise. You cannot calculate Him. You cannot coordinate events in history with God's actions, you see?

"So if the book of Revelation is apocalyptic, looking forward, those early chapters in Genesis are apocalyptic, looking backward. They look backward from God's angle, from the angle of the Creator, not the angle of the actual process. Therefore, you cannot have a one-to-one relation between what Genesis says and what we find in actual science."

What Torrance is saying here in part is that Genesis is true; but it's presented from a divinely oriented space-time perspective rather than our earthbound vision. To catch a glimpse of what it must be like to view Genesis from God's viewpoint, then, you might first imagine human time as an extremely long sidewalk.

If you stand on the sidewalk, you can't see the beginning or the end of it; in fact, it seems endless. But if somehow you can reach a vantage point well above the sidewalk, you can see all its configurations as it stretches out in front of you and behind you. You can see where it begins and ends, what's beyond it and around it, and how the different sections of the sidewalk relate to one another in the context of the whole. But only a little of this "divine" perspective is available to your sight if you're firmly planted on the ground.

Now let's return to the concept of light. Light, as Torrance said, is first in order of creation, both according to ancient Genesis and modern science. But there's much more to light and its relationship to theological truth than that. For one thing, light is *impartial*—and so is God's grace.

To illustrate, Torrance says, "Suppose you're driving along in a car at fifty miles per hour. You have one friend who's got a rifle, and another who has a flashlight—or what we call in Scotland a 'torch.'

"Now, the chap with the rifle fires a bullet out of his gun, and the bullet leaves the gun at a certain rate. So the bullet is traveling at that rate *plus* the rate of the car, which is fifty miles per hour. That's common sense, and that's also Newtonian science.

"As for the light, it leaves the flashlight at the speed of light. But the speed at which the light travels is *not* that speed plus the speed of the car. It's only the speed of light. And that is *not* common sense.

"This is the revolutionary thing about relativity theory: Light behaves in the same way all over the universe. It's impartial to everyone. But also, isn't this what Jesus said when He taught, 'God shines His sunlight on the just and the unjust alike?' So you see, the physical behavior of light tells us something about the grace of God, who is perfect Light. God loves all men equally, and that is most difficult to understand."

Still another characteristic of light, Torrance says—one which is directly related to the first—is that it's *constant*. "We need a constant in the universe. We've seen that all bodies in motion are defined in terms of space and time, and space and time are defined in terms of light. So if light is variable, then the whole universe is in chaos. But if light is constant, then you've got order throughout the whole universe.

"Now, that also tells us something about God. God is invariant in His love. If God is love, that is the center of all order. God is utterly faithful, and that's the center of everything, and something we can always rely upon."

When Torrance begins to probe a concept like this, the implications seem almost endless. He goes on to point out: "Light is invisible, and so is God. We know today that you can't see light. You only see what is lit up by light.

"One day I was visiting a meteorological station in Dundee, where light signals are received from satellites to give us the picture of the cloud cover that is on television every day. I said to them, 'Show me where the signals come in, please?' When they did so, I took a bit of paper and shoved it across to where the signals would be, and a spot of light appeared on the paper. I couldn't see the light, but I could see where the paper was lit up by the light.

"In the same way, you can't see God. But you can see what is lit up by the light of God."

Torrance then goes on to argue that God has "shone his light into the world in the face of Jesus. There He translates His light into a human life, and that human life you can see."

Illustrations like these, Torrance says, show that modern scientific ideas can give us a better grasp of the Gospel than was ever possible in the past.

But this is just a simple example of the way that Thomas Torrance draws parallels and relationships between theology and science. More often, he can be found elucidating much deeper concepts for crowded auditoriums filled with physicists and other scientists.

For example, he was asked to give a lecture on God and the physical world in Switzerland on the hundredth anniversary of Einstein's birth. "The others were all scientists of some kind, physicists and cosmologists, and I said to them, 'Look, I'd rather speak on God and the contingent world.' They said yes. So I tried to show that the more profoundly we get into the nature of the universe, the more the universe cries out for God. In doing so, I took to pieces the so-called steady-state theory of the universe."

Unknown to Torrance, however, a leading advocate of the steady-state theory was present in the audience. When the professor had finished his talk, this man jumped up, and, as Torrance recalls, "My heart failed me."

But far from disagreeing with the theologian, the scientist told him, "You're right. I've always been an atheist, but I can no longer be an atheist."

Then they proceeded to discuss Einstein's concept of God, tied that discussion in to Spinoza's thought and finally agreed that there is an element of transcendence in Einstein's understanding of God.

After this discussion, the president of the American Academy of Science stood up and said he agreed with Torrance and the steady-state physicist. "I've always been an agnostic, but I can no longer be an agnostic," he announced.

Encounters like these are commonplace in the world in which Thomas Torrance travels. And at those points where theoretical physics and theology converge, few can match his facility with the concepts of space and time.

At the heart of his system of thought is a firm belief in a universe that possesses "contingent rationality." This means, first of all, that he believes that scientific evidence supports the position that God created the world out of nothing, with an existence and a pattern different from God.

"Since the universe has its own pattern and order, if I want to understand the plants I can't do that by theology," he explains. "I just have to examine the plants. But the more I examine the plants, the more I see there's no self-explanation for them. So the more I understand the universe, I find that I must conclude that the universe can be rational only if there is a Transcendent Ground—or God—which gives it rationality. The universe, then, is 'contingent' because it depends on something beyond itself. It's not self-explaining, self-upholding, self-sufficient."

So, entering the complex mind of Thomas Torrance can present some stimulating, even overwhelming challenges to the intellect. But perhaps the most rewarding challenges are those presented to the heart.

Professor Torrance is a man who can spar on a conceptual level with the finest minds in science and religion. But he is most interested in communicating that eternal message of the Incarnation, which is the "axis in the universe" around which his own life revolves.

So an evening spent with Professor Thomas Torrance is quite unlike most other informal meetings or conversations. If you happen to agree with his Christian assumptions, you're likely to go away intellectually stimulated and spiritually inspired. If you disagree with his world view, you're at least sure to have some serious new thoughts to ponder. But regardless of your religious orientation, you'll be challenged to think and act from the deepest roots of your being—and that's the point at which real progress in religion begins.

18

Nikkyo Niwano
Founder of Rissho Kosei-Kai

Although a person may seem to be an "overnight success"—
especially if he is young or relatively new to a field—great accomplishment usually requires long preparation. In other words, great
achievements in life are almost always the culmination of years of
hard work, personal sacrifice and self-discipline. And the necessity
of a long apprenticeship is particularly evident in the realm of social and spiritual progress.

One of the best examples of this principle of long-term preparation and perseverance can be found in the life of a Japanese pickle
peddler and milkman, Nikkyo Niwano. He rose from the humblest
peasant origins to become one of the major Buddhist leaders of
his own country and also an internationally recognized advocate
of world peace. So Niwano's life is a testimony to the value of
total commitment to a cause and an example to men and women
of any faith who desire to see their beliefs transformed into powerful, beneficial action and superior achievement.

Born into a farming family, Nikkyo Niwano was the second of
six children. He and his parents and siblings lived under the same
roof with another family—a total of fourteen people—in the mountainous Japanese village of Suganuma. Most people born under
such circumstances live and die in obscurity. They may be supremely important to a small circle of blood relations and loved
ones. But it's unlikely that they will scale the heights of international fame and history-making accomplishment.

Something about Nikkyo Niwano was different, however.

It may have been his basically sensitive, peace-loving personality. Or as he puts it in his autobiography, *Lifetime Beginner*, "People who praise me say that I am straightforward and cheerful. Others say that I am gullible and easygoing to a fault. Both assessments are accurate. But I can add another: I do not like to quarrel or fight. Later, I learned peace and harmony as Buddhist ideals, but they were a part of my emotional make-up from childhood."

But there was more to it than that. A sweet, sensitive nature alone may lead a person to a happy and satisfied, but rather ordinary, uneventful life. Greatness depends on an extra ingredient. In Niwano's case, that something extra was his unequivocal commitment to hard work. When he had left his village to find employment in the outside world, his father advised him "to look for a job where the work was back-breaking, the hours long and the pay low." The idea behind this counsel was that such effort would give him "neither the time nor the money to go wrong."

The immediate results of his willingness to work netted Niwano a series of job offers. "Working hard and long was a principle with me," Niwano writes. "I did not even rest on holidays. I realize that people today might consider my attitude odd, nor do I recommend that it be followed by everyone. Nonetheless, I was gaining in an important respect."

The personal gain he experienced was that he was exchanging his labor, as he says, for *more* than money. He greatly valued the "positive, aggressive spirit" that he developed in these early years —a spirit that stood him in good stead when more important tasks in the religious and social realm came his way in later life.

But his character was just beginning to develop the buds that would come into full bloom years later, and his life's work was not yet a speck on his personal horizon. In retrospect, his gradual personal development was exactly the kind of slow, measured movement that Niwano always preferred. He said later: "Steady progress is the most important thing in life. The Buddha teaches that it is not the person who walks in the Buddha's shadow that is closest to him, but the person who fervently seeks the way. . . . [But] even though the course may be slow, it is vital that daily progress in self-refinement be made. The person must be farther along the way tomorrow than he is today, and still farther along the way the day after tomorrow than he will be tomorrow."

The first tiny steps toward a religious expression of his developing inner character traits came in his early years when he had just started his lifelong commitment to hard work. One of his first employers, a Mr. Yoshitaro Ishihara, was a member of the Organization of National Faith and Virtue (Wagakuni Shintoku-sha), a group that focused on Chinese fortune-telling systems.

Niwano became mildly interested in this organization's beliefs—particularly the notion that all aspects of life can be interpreted and predicted according to certain rules based on the locations and movements of various physical things and people. At first, he thought it was silly to believe in such a system. But then, as a lark, he decided to try it out. To his surprise, he found he was right in interpreting and applying this group's rules in about 85 percent of all cases in which he attempted it.

Despite the seeming success of this method, Niwano's brush with the spiritual realm didn't really impress him at this point. So he put any explicit religious involvement on the back burners of his mind for the time being. But still, the basic traits of character that he had been developing as a child continued to blossom as he moved through young adulthood.

Even when he entered the Japanese Navy in 1926, he remembered and affirmed his roots, which were so firmly imbedded in compassion and sensitivity for the needs of others. "One of the greatest harvests from my military experience was a reinforcement of my philosophy of nonviolence," he writes. "Corporal punishment was an everyday affair, but in my entire military career I never struck anyone subordinate to me."

But it was only after his discharge from the service that his inner development and his ultimate mission in life began to come together. One of the greatest turning points in Niwano's life came just after he married his cousin Sai (later called Naoko).

Soon their first child, a little daughter, was born. But only a month after her birth, the girl suffered a severe inflammation of her inner ear. On the advice of a friend, Niwano and his wife decided to seek help from a woman named Umeno Tsunaki, who practiced a form of Buddhist faith healing, which involves strict physical training and personal discipline.

Following Mrs. Tsunaki's orders, he began to go to her religious observances every night and to pray regularly. To his surprise, his daughter improved steadily—and, in fact, had her bandages removed on the exact day that Mrs. Tsunaki had predicted.

The result was that Niwano took the woman a small gift of money and asked her to take him on as one of her students. She agreed, and his life as a committed follower of Buddhism began.

At first he concentrated on prayers and other contemplative devotional exercises. But then he progressed to more challenging practices: One of these was the "cold-water bath." He would go outside in the dead of winter, wearing nothing but a thin white kimono, and then would pour frigid well water over his head as he repeated various Buddhist litanies. The idea of this exercise was to try to move closer to oneness with the Buddha by reaching the first rung on the ladder of spiritual concentration called the *samadhi*.

He also severely restricted his diet to uncooked cereals and other raw foods. Asceticism became a way of life for him in this early period. And as he delved into different approaches to Buddhism, his religious commitment became the absolute priority in his life—a priority which even prompted him at one point to abandon his family for a period of ten years.

Niwano's movement into this singleminded commitment was gradual but total. During this formative period, one of the most decisive influences on him was his discovery of the Lotus Sutra, a sacred scripture of Buddhism. He began to study this text regularly and was especially impressed by two of the teachings he encountered: (1) "the way of compassion of the bodhisattva—helping others and serving everyone in the world—is the true meaning of Buddhism"; and (2) "the ability of the lay believer both to save and to be saved."

These two principles—compassion for others and the power of the lay believer—became his permanent guiding lights as he assumed leadership in the Japanese Buddhist community. And all his decisions and actions—including any divine revelations he felt he had received—were always tested against the teachings of the Lotus Sutra. If they conflicted with those teachings, the written text would take priority, and the experience would be disregarded.

Because of Niwano's strong, individualistic Buddhist beliefs, he found that he had trouble expressing himself with completely authentic spirituality in the existing religious groups with which he came into contact. So he decided, with one of his closest colleagues, Mrs. Masa Naganuma, to form a new Buddhist group, the Rissho Kosei-Kai, on March 5, 1938.

Rissho means "establishing the teaching of the true Law [that is, the Lotus Sutra] in the world." *Ko,* of *Kosei,* refers to "mutual exchange of thought among people of faith, that is, the principle of spiritual unity among different human beings." *Sei* means the "perfection of the personality and attainment of buddhahood." Mrs. Naganuma—who came to be known as Myoko Sensei, or "Teacher Myoko"—died a few years later, and the mantle of supreme leadership fell to Niwano alone.

Niwano's growing involvement in Buddhist activities caused him to neglect his business interests, and often he hardly made enough money to pay his bills and support his family. Also, the increasingly long amounts of time he spent away from his wife and six children caused severe marital strains. Finally, he was ordered by other leaders in his fledgling organization to live apart from his wife and children for an indefinite period of time.

So committed was he to his work and beliefs that he agreed and took the painful step of separating himself from his loved ones. He sent them to his family's home in the country, and as wrenching as the separation was, he abided by the decision of his Rissho Kosei-Kai colleagues—for the incredible period of ten years!

During that period he refused to talk to his wife and children when he came into contact with them at family functions, such as funerals; and the extent of his communication with them was an occasional brief letter.

In retrospect, Niwano concluded in his autobiography, "By being separated from my family for ten years of struggle and search, I came to realize that faith is real only when it embraces the whole family." Now he frequently expresses remorse at the pain he caused his wife and children. But somehow they managed to pick up the relationship and begin again after that ten-year hiatus. And he interprets the preservation of his family ties after such intense pressures as a divine miracle.

With such rigorous personal preparation and self-sacrifice having honed him to the sharpest edge of devotion and commitment,

Niwano was ready for the greatest challenge of his life: He began to assume national and, eventually, international leadership in promoting religious and social issues. And as in the early days of his life, compassion for others was the overriding principle in his actions.

Here are some of his achievements:

• His Buddhist lay organization, Rissho Kosei-Kai, has become the largest Buddhist organization in the world, with a membership of 4.6 million.

• Despite opposition in his own country, he helped establish the Union of the New Religious Organizations in Japan in 1951, in an effort to promote cooperation between different religious groups. The next year, this group was accepted by the Japan Religions League, a more established interfaith group. And in 1969 Niwano was elected chairman of the League.

• He has traveled regularly to other nations to promote interreligious—and consequently, social and political—understanding between different nations and peoples. For example, he met with top Buddhist leaders in India and worked behind the scenes in an attempt to promote a commitment to universal equality. Also, when he met with Pope Paul VI in 1965, the Pope, holding his hand, told Niwano: "I know what you are doing for interreligious cooperation. It is very wonderful. Please continue to promote this wonderful movement."

• Despite Vietnamese governmental opposition, he traveled around South Vietnam during the Vietnam War, where he distributed relief packages and shared encouraging words with the poor and oppressed.

• In 1970 he took the lead in sponsoring the first World Conference on Religion and Peace, which brought leaders of every major faith and nation to Kyoto, Japan. There was an abundance of coolness and skepticism in Japan toward this meeting, but Niwano worked hard to overcome the criticism—so hard that his health began to suffer. But the reservoirs of self-discipline and willingness to sacrifice personal considerations carried him through to a successful conclusion.

"The first World Conference on Religion and Peace was held with great success," he wrote afterwards in *Lifetime Beginner*. "Dr. Eugene Carson Blake of the World Council of Churches attended, as did representatives from the Vatican. Among the communist nations, the Soviet Union, Poland, East Germany, Romania, Bulgaria, and Outer Mongolia were represented. "Encounter is the essential starting point for all human relations. Only when encounters occur can discussions take place. And only from discussions can understanding, trust, and friendship be forthcoming. The road we must travel in the future is long, but meetings of people of religion from all over the world, in the hope of achieving one great common goal, are steps in the right direction."

• A second World Conference on Religion and Peace was held in Belgium in 1974, and there the discussions frequently heated up as touchy topics were aired. Bishop Peter Sarpong of Ghana argued for the right of resistance to oppression by African blacks, while American and European representatives disagreed with this position. A Vietnamese delegate complained about continuing violence in his country, despite the supposed advent of peace. And Indian representatives supported their government's nuclear tests, while the Japanese criticized that decision.

But in spite of the disagreements and arguments, the significant thing was that important questions of violence and war and peace were being aired—were being *discussed,* rather than fought about on a battlefield. So, even if most issues weren't resolved, those on opposing sides at least understood each other a little better.

• In 1979 Nikkyo Niwano was awarded the Templeton Foundation Prize for Progress in Religion, which carried a cash award of one hundred and sixty-eight thousand dollars, in recognition of his work for interfaith understanding and peace.

So Nikkyo Niwano's monumental efforts toward peace and understanding among religious groups over the years have earned him just recognition. And his life stands as a challenge to men and women of all faiths who also want to promote peace and love outside their local religious communities.

His outward accomplishments have become a consistent testimony to the deep inner convictions that motivate him. He has, indeed, become a living example of that passage in his beloved Lotus Sutra, which reads: "Then from the midst of the Precious Stupa there came a loud voice, praising and saying: 'Excellent!

Excellent! World-honored Shakyamuni! Thou art able to preach to the great assembly the Wonderful Law-Flower Sutra of universal and great wisdom, by which bodhisattvas are instructed and which the Buddhas guard and mind."

19

Ralph Wendell Burhoe
Founder of *Zygon*, a Journal of Science and Religion

Two factors are especially important in the effort to achieve progress in any field, including both religion and science. One is the ability to ask the right kind of provocative questions. And the other is the establishment of open forums of discussion, so that researchers from a variety of backgrounds can present their findings and hone them to a sharp edge in informed debate.

The 1980 winner of the Templeton Prize for Progress in Religion, Dr. Ralph Wendell Burhoe, is unique in that he has played a decisive role in promoting *both* of these ingredients of progress.

Burhoe is regarded by his colleagues as both a scientist and theologian, and the work he has done in those fields has won him significant recognition on several fronts. Sometimes the questions he raises—such as a theory he has posited suggesting that religion may play an important role in human revolution—have provoked considerable controversy. But his reputation rests primarily on the fact that he helped establish the highly regarded scholarly periodical, *Zygon,* a Journal of Religion and Science, at the Meadville/ Lombard Theological School's Center for Advanced Study in Chicago, where he was Professor of Theology and Science. In addition, he was one of the founders of the Institute on Religion in an Age of Science and of the Center for Advanced Study in Religion and Science.

In more recent years perhaps the most important position he has taken is to call in a warm and loving, but still quite urgent, way for a return to religious values. He believes this development is absolutely necessary if we hope to achieve lasting scientific and technological progress.

"Religion is an essential part of our culture," he explains. "It is central to our values. But people today are saying that religion is no longer important: It's not relevant. We're now in a terrible age of lack of faith because we don't have anything which we can believe in and which will still allow us to believe in what we learn in school.

"Children of theologians are going to school and learning to despise theology. I happen to know some cases. That's been true all this century, but it shouldn't be. The children of scientists don't go to school and learn that physics is no good and untrue."

The implications of the present inadequacy of our religious beliefs—and the prospect that our youngsters will be even less believing in the future—are ominous, Burhoe says. "I don't pretend to know whether we're going to have an atomic holocaust and a decimation of the world population, along with the possible end of human life," he says. "But all kinds of things are possible now that never were possible before because of the terrible powers that we have in our hands. What is critical is a lack of internalized respect for the social order and respect for the needs of others. This is the result of the absence of a religion, which generates powerful convictions of God's sovereignty and of our duties."

In light of the present lack of religious values to control the uses of our proliferating scientific advances, Burhoe sees two possible scenarios for the future:

• The "worst case scenario" is that "Western liberal civilization will go out because it can't control itself. We may break up into small groups, with very powerful, totalitarian, semi-military regimes running them. I see various currents that seem to be leading that way, including Hitler, Mussolini and Stalin."

• The "ideal way," in contrast, might be for the church, led by a "marvelous Pope," to band together with other religions and promote an intellectually credible synthesis of their traditions with the scientific tradition.

"Then," Burhoe says, "you would have a synthesis that could

be believed, and one which was pertinent and relevant to the main issues that religion should be concerned with—namely, the worship of the Lord of history, and service to Him, and hope through Him. If we proclaimed that what we call God is revealed in the scientific evidence for the forces generating and selecting our lives and the requirements they lay upon us, it would turn around the minds of the scientists who say they can't speak with God; turn around the minds of the diplomats who don't believe in God; turn around the minds of the businessmen who live as though there were no God."

When he considers what he thinks the world could be—and then looks at where he's afraid it's going—Ralph Burhoe, usually a reserved, soft-spoken man, doesn't hesitate to say where he stands. "It seems to me to be quite clear that there is an ultimate reality system that is our Lord and Master, and whose rules and promises should order our lives. Not only that, we should love and trust and have hope in this system. And equally, we should love and have hope for our fellow humans."

Burhoe is a thoroughgoing intellectual, and most of the great adventures of his life take place in his mind and in scholarly interactions with his theological and scientific colleagues. But at the same time, he has a passionate concern for the future of humanity. And he's deeply worried that we are failing to take those steps which will preserve us as a progressive society that nurtures rather than oppresses the human spirit.

Much of his concern is rooted in his concept of the evolutionary process, which has resulted, he believes, in a gradual improvement of human religious thought and morality. "One has to suppose that religion, like language and various technologies and social forms and morals and other things, evolved gradually," he says.

There are several ways in which Burhoe believes that man's religious orientation helped humans evolve to a high state. On one level, for example, there is the social or community element that is central to all religions. "Religious rules were necessary for preserving good order in the social system and in our feelings and motivations toward one another. Without religion, men never would have become men. So religion had a special role in enabling us to transcend our genetic limitations of showing altruism only toward close kin. Without that spiritual influence, we couldn't have had larger societies, and hence we couldn't be human."

Burhoe even goes so far as to hypothesize: "Religion is indeed the missing link between ape man and civilized humans. This is a hypothesis that isn't widely accepted yet, and it may be broken. But I have so far found that it is the most probable way of accounting for the emergence of humanity as a system of social life that transcends the genetic bond."

More specifically, Burhoe believes, "We are so constructed and designed that we seek for God. That is, we want to know what is our source—that upon which we are dependent, that which created us, and that which is, indeed, the Judge and Determiner of our destiny. This is a part of human nature, and I believe it's a very stable part because this search is built into our brains as well as into our cultures and genes. The object of this search is the Ultimate Reality that many people talk about."

It's important to note at this point, however, that Burhoe is not arguing in favor of some sort of "religious gene" in the human body. Rather, he believes "there are many genes which make us religious creatures, just as there are many genes that make us able to speak language."

In other words, it's a *composite* of many genes together with a cultural heritage that makes us religious beings. So there is a complex of genes in each of us that provides a religious predisposition, he believes. And those genes, in turn, can only reach their complete potential in a hospitable cultural context.

But unfortunately, in our own time something seems to have gone wrong with the cultural and genetic balance that can produce a beneficial religious experience. Burhoe says we have "abused our ecosystem. We have neglected true brotherhood. We are possessed by selfishness for our own society or our individual family life, without being ready to give ourselves to the needs of the total human community. I think that this development is highly dangerous. Forgetting that there is a system of Reality, which is our sovereign and our savior, is the primary danger."

What is the answer to this dilemma, in Burhoe's view?

Perhaps the best statement of his position on what should be done can be found in the closing words of "True Spirituality in the Light of the Sciences," a paper he presented to a Unitarian group in Toledo, Ohio, in 1981:

"Our rapidly changing, twentieth-century . . . world is caught up in the most innovative and disruptive . . . transition in history. The disruption requires more time for the search for better-adapted spiritual insights. The scientific-technological environment requires a spiritual understanding or theology adapted to scientific understandings of reality. The advance of mankind to find a more harmonious and stable future . . . depends upon the advance of religious doctrine and education to fulfill new spiritual needs."

Ralph Burhoe will probably always attract only a small following because of the complexity of his thought and the unusual nature of some of his theories, which often differ markedly from conventional religious belief. But he has served as a spiritual catalyst by encouraging scientists and theologians to think more seriously about each other's fields. And he provided the common ground, as the first editor of *Zygon,* for them to have dialogue with one another and, on occasion, to find common ground in building bridges over their disagreements.

So, as study into the relationship between science and religion moves into ever deeper waters in the upcoming years, the captains of those future research projects are likely to remember with some fondness the contributions of their gentle, retiring, but totally committed predecessor, Ralph Wendell Burhoe.

20

Dame Cicely Saunders
Founder of the Modern
Hospice Movement

Some people discover their calling as a result of a single illuminating event. For others, there may be no single turning point, but rather a series of seemingly connected incidents and insights that appear so strongly directed that there is no denying the ultimate goal or purpose.

It was just such a pattern of events that shaped the career and spiritual perceptions of a young Englishwoman, Cicely Saunders, and set her on a path that led her from a wartime student nurse to one of the world's foremost experts in the care of the dying.

Largely because of Dame Cicely's work, the word "hospice" no longer simply means a place for travelers to rest. Nor is it a catch-all word for dismal places where people go to die. Rather, modern hospices are for patients who don't respond to ordinary cures. These way stations on the last leg of a life's journey specialize in supportive services. They cater to the physical, psychological, social and spiritual care for dying persons and their families. And they have evolved into comprehensive centers of medical aid and comfort, including special hospital facilities and home care arrangements, largely through the unflagging efforts of Dame Cicely.

Yet it was almost by accident that young Cicely got involved in medicine at all. When World War II broke out, she dropped out of her undergraduate studies at Oxford to become a nurse. But even though she received an honors certificate from nursing school, Cicely was unable to continue nursing because of a bad back. So she returned to Oxford and got a war degree and a social science diploma.

While pursuing her practical social work studies, Cicely, a recently committed Christian, began to search for some ultimate mission or life's work. She recalls that she put this problem in God's hands at just about the time that the Japanese surrendered in World War II.

"Something about the words 'unconditional surrender' just flipped a switch for me," she said. "I remember saying to God, 'I've been emotional at times and very intellectual at others, but it hasn't really been real. Please, could it be real this time?' "

A strong feeling came over her—a feeling which she took as a direct divine response. She felt that someone was telling her, "I've done it all— you only have to accept."

After that, it seemed as though her life turned around 180 degrees. "Instead of battling against the wind, the wind was behind me."

Yet she still had no inkling of precisely what her life's work would be. And she wouldn't know until she began to work directly with the patients who would change her life.

It was at the Royal Marsden, then called the Royal Cancer Hospital, in London that Cicely first dealt with patients who were terminally ill. Her story from that point actually becomes the story of her encounters with patients, many of whom were instrumental in setting the final direction for her life. They instilled in her the confidence that she could do the job; they gave her a belief that the often discouraging work with the terminally ill was meaningful; and they showed her that there was a great deal more to be accomplished.

Cicely came to feel that she had to find a way to help dying patients through their final moments. She wanted, somehow, to make those last breaths meaningful, quiet, and permeated by an atmosphere of love—not anguish or loneliness. If a person is alone during a final illness, she decided, then perhaps a social worker or nurse could provide some companionship and love.

On the other hand, if the dying person had a family, the medical professional could take the initiative to get those loved ones

more involved. Cicely's growing convictions about the importance
of the presence of the family were bolstered by an experience she
had with a family whose father was dying of terminal cancer.

The man, a personal friend of hers, slowly realized that his disease would result in his death. But he resolved to say nothing to
his relatives until he had learned to face and overcome his own
fears.

Knowing now what he had to do, this man got up the courage
to ask his doctor about his condition a few days later. The doctor
unwillingly confirmed that he was indeed going to die from his illness. But the patient, far from being depressed, experienced a sudden relief from the long period of uncertainty. And his family was
also relieved that they no longer had to carry on a well-meaning
charade to avoid talking about the inevitable.

Now, with the truth finally revealed, they were all able to take
care of practical family matters in a frank way. The patient attended to all the details of his own funeral and other final business
matters. And Cicely Saunders was able to help the other family
members care for him more effectively in his last three weeks.

As a result, they were able to spend their final few weeks at
home together in an atmosphere of great love and honest sharing.
When he finally died at home, the family was able to look back on
the experience with pride and satisfaction.

This patient hadn't been an actively religious man. But he
moved closer in his final days toward an understanding of God.
His final illness seemed to bring out the best in the man, as far as
Cicely was concerned. And Cicely saw that a great part of the
richness of the experience resulted from the entire family's ability
to share in the responsibilities of his care. So her experience with
this patient and his loved ones helped her still further to formulate
her philosophy of dealing with the totality of the needs and problems of the terminally ill.

Yet there was one other patient who represented perhaps the
most significant turning point for Cicely's eventual life's work. He
helped her to see more clearly than anyone else the breadth of the
contribution she might be able to make.

This patient was a Polish Jew from the Warsaw ghetto, David
Tasma, who had been an outpatient with an incurable illness. She
had known him for several months as a result of a few outpatient

visits, when the disease suddenly took a turn for the worse and he had to be admitted to another hospital.

David, an agnostic, was completely alone, and he needed desperately to sort out his life in those last few weeks. So Cicely visited him regularly and tried her best to help him through the end.

"I want what is in your mind," David said. "And what is in your heart."

So Cicely responded and offered what he had asked of her—communication with the soul. This may not have been quite in line with what many nursing, medical, or social work schools advocate about keeping a certain detachment from the patient. But Cicely knew there had to be another side to the medical approach to death. There had to be something more than just techniques for controlling pain through drugs and for applying various medical skills.

From David, Cicely learned that pain is not only physical, mental and social—it has spiritual dimensions as well. Even though she and David were far apart in their religious beliefs, Cicely came to understand that he was in a position to teach her a great deal about death. "He made his peace with the God of his fathers," she says. They talked of ways that people in his condition could be better cared for; and together they shared a vision of giving the terminally ill the best treatment possible.

Just before his death, David gave Cicely a very concrete commitment to continue their vision: He left her a gift of £500, which he wanted her to use in a very specific way to realize their new dream.

"I'll be a window in your home," he said. And sure enough, years later, she used that gift to pay for the front window in her history-making hospice in London, St. Christopher's.

But that's getting a little ahead of our story. At the time of David Tasma's death, she still didn't have a clear-cut picture of her life's mission. But she did have a definite starting point and some new goals.

So she decided to commit herself totally to the treatment of pain and care for the dying. An important preliminary step in realizing this goal was to gain experience at places where work was being conducted on the treatment of pain and on the special needs of the dying. So she spent three years as a nurse-volunteer twice a week at one of the older hospices, St. Luke's. Cicely was considering continuing to pursue these goals as a nurse—until she talked with a surgeon who nudged her in another direction.

"There is so much more to be learned about pain," he said. "We haven't even really looked at it yet. You'll only be frustrated unless you do it properly. So do it as a doctor."

This same surgeon helped Cicely Saunders return in 1951 to St. Thomas' Hospital, where she had received her training in nursing and in medical social work. But this time she came back, at age thirty-three, as a medical student with a mission.

She graduated with honors in 1957 and continued to study how drugs could be used in the treatment of patients with terminal illness at St. Mary's Medical School. Also, she was involved in the day-do-day care of forty-five patients at St. Joseph's Hospice as part of the practical applications of her knowledge. This background helped her in pioneering the better use of morphine and other drugs for the terminally ill. With these techniques a dying individual could stay lucid and able to relate well to his loved ones right up to the end, even as he remained relatively pain-free.

As she pursued her clinical research, she didn't lose that special feeling for her patients that she had been developing as a nurse and social worker. Her natural empathy for those who were suffering their final illness is especially apparent in her work as a doctor with another Polish patient in 1960.

This man, whose name was Antoni, was an electronic engineer, and he was under her care for the seven months he stayed at the hospice. But she really got to know him well only in the last three weeks of his life, after his condition suddenly turned much worse.

Antoni realized that his time was drawing near, and when Dr. Saunders came in to see him one day, he grabbed her hand and kissed it. "Thank you, Doctor," he said. "Not just for your pills, but for your heart."

The doctor recalls that at that point her world was "unmade." She tried to respond, but she choked up and simply couldn't utter the words she wanted to say. This marked the beginning of an intensely close spiritual and emotional relationship—the kind of involvement that doctors frequently believe they must avoid if they want to give a patient the best care. But with the dying, Dr.

Saunders had long since found that the usual medical rules often don't apply.

The next day, while she was visiting him, Antoni asked abruptly, "Doctor, am I really going to die?"

"Yes," she answered. It didn't seem appropriate to add any extra words, so she remained silent and waited for him to continue.

"Long?"

"No." It wouldn't be long, and she saw no point in pretending it would.

Antoni paused for a moment and then continued. "Was it hard for you to tell me that?"

"Yes," Dr. Saunders replied. "It was."

"It's hard to be told, but it's hard to tell too. Thank you."

Over the next three weeks Dr. Saunders went to see Antoni often. At first he seemed to resist the idea that he was nearing the end. "I do not *want* to die. I do not *want* to die," he repeated.

Dr. Saunders, too, could not bear the thought of losing him, because they had become such close friends. "I prayed, 'Please, let him stay a bit longer,'" she says.

When it was getting especially hard for them to face the truth that his death was inevitable and not far away, Dr. Saunders suddenly awoke from a dream one night with an insight. "I found that my heart had gone quiet. I realized that Antoni was tired and that I couldn't ask him to stay."

She was content now that the matter was in God's hands, and she knew she couldn't hold on to him any longer. When she saw him again, she said, "Why do you look so sad?"

"How should I look? Amused?" he asked.

But as the end drew near, Antoni's perspective changed too. He no longer asked to be saved from death. "I only want what is right," he said finally.

Their last five days together were spent in marvelous quiet and peace. The last time Dr. Saunders saw Antoni alive, he looked up at her and gave her a tremendously amused smile. At first it puzzled her: They had been going through so much together for the past few weeks that she wondered what he could possibly be thinking. But then she saw what was happening.

"I realized that he had been smiling because for the first time he was seeing all the answers," she explains. "I realized that he saw he was going to be all right—and I was going to be all right too. He was joyful and liberated."

Even that revelation didn't totally relieve the pain of his death, however. Although Dr. Saunders was heavily burdened with work, she could not think or do anything immediately after Antoni died. She took a few days off to sort things out and to try to understand the effect of Antoni's friendship on her. Even when she came back to the hospice a few days later, she couldn't bear the thought of entering his ward again and seeing someone else in his bed.

"Lord," she said. "I can't go in. It hurts too much."

But she had to enter. And as she walked in the ward, the first thing her eyes focused on was the crucifix on the wall. "It helped me to see that symbol—it was so terribly important. As I went round the hospice wards, it was the crucifix that would hold me together."

It was experiences like this that molded Cicely Saunders personally and professionally and led her to open a new kind of facility for the terminally ill in 1967. And appropriately enough, in light of her experience with Antoni and so many others, it was called "St. Christopher's Hospice," after the old man who, according to tradition, was supposed to have helped carry people across a treacherous river.

It seems that one dark and stormy night a child knocked on his door and asked, "Christopher, take me across."

So Christopher put the child on his shoulders and waded into the water. But as he walked along, the child seemed to get heavier and heavier. When he looked up to see what was the matter, he saw that there was also a cross on his back. Christopher was carrying the Christ child, with the weight and sorrows of the world on his back in addition to that small body. But even with this tremendous burden, the old laborer realized that he was receiving strength from Christ to enable him to continue to the other side.

Dame Cicely Saunders—as she has been known since receiving this title from the Crown in 1980—understands well the weight that old Christopher was carrying. And like Christopher, her own spiritual resources and relationship with Christ have enabled her to bear the great burdens of the terminally ill which are piled on her day after day.

She has managed not only to meet the draining demands of individual patients, like Antoni, David Tasma and others, but also to spread the exciting new hospice concept to many nations and hundreds of similar facilities around the world. St. Christopher's has become synonymous with modern hospice care and is a center both for patient treatment and also for teaching and research. The emphasis continues to be on combining scientific use of pain-killing and other drugs and other late medical developments with a warm atmosphere that stresses the involvement of the whole family in the dying experience.

For her work in this field—and, as she stresses, for the work of her medical teams—Dame Cicely has received a plethora of awards and prizes. She was given the O.B.E. in 1967, the D.B.E. in 1980, and was elected a member of the Royal College of Physicians in 1968. She also holds honorary doctorates from Yale, Columbia and other universities.

And in 1981 she was awarded the Templeton Prize for Progress in Religion, along with a grant of two hundred thousand dollars, which she has used for projects at St. Christopher's. In her characteristically direct and honest fashion, she says, "I got my prize not for being kind but for making this a respectable part of medicine and proving that pain can be relieved by the detailed scientific studies carried out by our Research Fellows."

But even as the honors continue to accumulate and the influence of St. Christopher's increases, Dame Cicely still retains that early feeling she developed as a nurse and social worker for the needs and sensitivities of her individual patients. To add her own personal touch at the hospice, she has hung bright, cheerful paintings created by her husband, the Polish artist Marian Bohusz. Also, as her patients are wheeled in for Sunday chapel service, she or one of her medical team greets each one intimately, for they know the patients' aches and pains and family relationships.

Just as David Tasma had said he would be a "window in your home," so Dame Cicely Saunders has become a window in the lives of many individuals. Most of them are no longer with us, but during their last journey they were able to see who they were and where they were going a little more clearly because of her transparent concern for them.

21

Billy Graham
Pioneer of New Methods
of Evangelism

We live in an age when communication in all forms has assumed overriding importance. From network television and radio news coverage, to special consumer cable TV services, to scientifically tested commercials and direct-mail appeals, we are caught up in the art of bombarding others with every conceivable message in every conceivable medium. For better or worse, mass communication appears destined to play a decisive role in shaping our thinking and actions in the years to come.

But even as the propagation of information proliferates at an accelerating pace, there are certain messages that remain distinct from all the others. These special communications may be presented with all the pizzazz and professionalism of the smoothest advertisement. But the point they are making is different: They contain the eternal Word of faith which is intended to change the lives of those who hear or see.

Of course, there's nothing new about propagating the Word of God throughout the world in the most effective and far-reaching ways possible. Jesus, in his "Great Commission" in Matthew 28:19–20, said: "Go therefore and make disciples of all nations, baptizing them in the name of the Father and of the Son and of the Holy Spirit, teaching them to observe all that I have commanded you; and lo, I am with you always, to the close of the age."

In the same vein, the Apostle Paul urged Timothy: ". . . preach the word, be urgent in season and out of season, convince, rebuke, and exhort, be unfailing in patience and in teaching." (2 Timothy 4:2)

The Christian church has always followed this principle of promoting evangelism. But the art of communicating the Word to large audiences has reached a kind of "state of the art" in the last few centuries with the rise of the evangelical Protestant revival movements.

It all began with Jonathan Edwards, who, though reportedly not a particularly powerful speaker, was nevertheless instrumental in sparking the Great Awakening in New England in the early eighteenth century. His secret was that he urged commitment from the pulpit to congregations whose members had already been primed by a sense of spiritual expectation and one-to-one evangelism. In a very real sense, it was his *timing,* preaching when spiritual sensitivities were high, that was the key to his evangelistic success.

Later preachers, like the Englishmen George Whitefield and John Wesley, were known to be more persuasive speakers who had a compelling style in the pulpit, as well as a sense of when God was working among the people. The same might be said of Charles Finney, who led American revivals in the early nineteenth century—movements of the Spirit which many historians feel resulted directly in the abolitionist movement and other reform efforts.

The tradition of swaying large audiences from the pulpit and platform continued into the early twentieth century with men like Dwight L. Moody and Billy Sunday. But then, in the mid-twentieth century, the style of evangelism changed dramatically, as did many other aspects of life. It was at that time that travel to various parts of the world became much faster and easier through the advent of jet carriers. Even more important, electronic devices appeared which could project sounds and pictures in huge auditoriums and over the airwaves instantaneously to millions of people.

The basic principle of evangelism, which is to reach the greatest number of people in the fastest, most efficient way, was still the

same. But the mode of transmitting the message had been drasti-
cally altered. And the man of the hour—God's man to communicate His message in the fast-moving style of the new era—was
a modest, unassuming American named Billy Graham.

There is no doubt that Graham fits perfectly into the style required by our high-powered modern communications media. Typically, he dresses in conservative three-piece suits and is surrounded by a staff of aides who keep him moving along on
schedule and insulate him from outside distractions that might di-
vert him from his work.

All in all—with his tall, handsome, athletic build and peren-
nially deep tan—he looks and operates as much like a top corporate executive or an established entertainment celebrity, as a
preacher of the Gospel. And there's good reason: He *is* an executive and a major celebrity. But his genius is that he has been able
to preserve a purity, authenticity and simplicity in his Gospel message, even as he makes such skillful use of every modern technique of mass communication.

If Billy had had his way as a child, though, he probably would
have ended up as a professional baseball player. Born in 1918 on
a farm near Charlotte, North Carolina, he was a church-going
youngster, but that was mainly the result of his Presbyterian parents' discipline. He was more interested in playing pranks, playing
ball and hanging out with his friends.

At sixteen he got a summer job selling brushes door to door,
and some of his innate abilities—harbingers of what was to come
later in the pulpit—emerged. The job struck a chord in Billy, and
before the season was over, he was the top salesman in North Carolina. Today, he believes that his ability to sell so well stemmed
from one factor: "I believed in the product!" he says.

That ability to be persuasive in putting across a message he
believed in has carried over to his present work. Or, as he says,
"Sincerity is the biggest part of selling anything—including the
Christian plan of salvation."

But Billy had a long, winding road to travel before he began to
"sell" from the pulpit and over the airwaves. His parents certainly
kept after him to go into the ministry. But he was still enamored
of baseball, especially after he spent one summer playing semipro-
fessional ball.

So they reached a compromise: He went to a Bible school in an area that was accessible to major-league training camps. He decided that if God wanted him to be a ball player, the opportunity should arise in that setting. If not, he would look elsewhere for his future occupation.

Soon, though, Billy began to give sermons in a local Baptist church, and he found himself losing interest in baseball. One thing led to another, and he was eventually ordained and became pastor of a Baptist church in Illinois.

It was at this point that he had his first serious exposure to evangelizing through far-reaching electronic communications. He convinced his church to sponsor a forty-five-minute radio broadcast which became quite popular in the area. Then, after a couple of years at this ministry, he left his church to work full time for the Youth for Christ evangelistic organization.

Gradually, Billy Graham moved into conducting revivals before increasingly large audiences, until finally, he burst onto the national scene with a highly successful series of evangelistic rallies in Los Angeles in 1949. Before long, his face and name were plastered over all the world's major magazines and newspapers.

And as the opportunities for broader ministry and evangelization appeared, Graham responded with the techniques and style of speaking that were best suited to get the message across. He reportedly became the first major evangelist to use the "lapel microphone" and the jet airplane in his "crusades." As he was in the process of mastering these modern-day devices, he held highly successful rallies in London (1954), Glasgow (1955), New York City (1957) and a variety of other far-flung locations. During his life, he has preached to more people than any other person in world history.

But this sort of fast-paced life takes its toll. Graham has had to be away from his family for weeks at a time, and it's only in recent years, after his children have grown up, that his wife, Ruth, has been able to accompany him regularly on his trips. In addition to the strain of family separation—which Graham tends to minimize in discussions with others—probably the most difficult problem he faces is the threat of overwork and the constant specter of fatigue.

"I feel that I'm in the best health of my entire life," Graham said recently. "But that doesn't mean I don't get fatigued. The thing that causes me the most trouble is jet lag. Flying from one coast to the other doesn't bother me so much. But when you fly to someplace far off, like Japan, that's eleven or twelve hours' difference. As I get older, I find that I'm getting more tired in my travel and my work.

"It's a schedule that can make you give out physically after a while," Billy concedes. "I still try to get eight hours of sleep each night, but lately I have so much more to do. My schedule is packed and my responsibilities are greater. Because I write most of my own work, nearly all my waking hours are spent studying and reading."

And there are other frustrations that have appeared along with the success of his evangelistic ministry. For one thing, he regrets not being able to keep in contact with old friends because of his tight travel schedule. Also, there are so many things he wants to do that he just can't fit into a twenty-four-hour day.

"Opportunities arise that I just can't take advantage of," he says. "I have no time, no strength, no ability to meet all the demands. For every engagement I take, there must be twenty-five I have to turn down. I just try to work it out and trust the Lord to take care of the consequences."

But despite the threat of fatigue and frustration, Billy Graham has spiritual staying power. What's his secret? His strength can be described in terms of four key inner resources:

• *The Bible:* "Bible reading is probably my greatest source of spiritual growth and strength," he says. "In recent years I've tried to read five Psalms and one chapter of Proverbs each day before breakfast. Then perhaps I will focus on one person in the Bible and study the qualities he possesses. For instance, I'll study the life of Abraham and see what lessons I can learn from his obedience."

• *Prayer:* "As you read the Scriptures, they lead you immediately into prayer," he says. "You can't read the Scriptures without seeing your own need for prayer. I pray as I read, and I pray alone. I pray propped up in bed at night or in the morning—there's no special position to be in when you pray. I would say that I'm praying almost full time. I pray about everything. Even as I speak, I pray, 'Lord, please help me to say the right thing.'"

Graham says he puts aside an hour in the morning and an hour in the evening to devote entirely to prayer. "In the evening my wife and I usually have our prayers together. One of us will read and expound on the Scriptures, and we'll comment on the Scriptures together. Then we'll pray. In the morning we have our private time, when we pray individually."

• *The faith of family and friends:* "My wife is my number-one counselor," Graham says. "She's about the only person I totally confide in. My children are all devoted Christians: My three daughters are all Bible teachers, and my son has recently been ordained. I draw spiritual nourishment from all of them.

"The team of people with whom I work is another great source of strength because I pray with them more than I do with anyone else. Some of them have been with me for thirty years. But really, you draw spiritual strength from almost anyone you meet who's a believer."

• *Pragmatic steps to reduce daily tensions and pressures:* While spiritual resources like Bible reading and prayer are of paramount importance in strengthening Graham's inner life and combating fatigue, he has discovered it's also important to cut down on his commitments. In other words, he tries to spend as much time as possible alone or in leisure activities.

"I'm trying to cut out those early-morning breakfasts—ones where I'm invited to speak—so I can be a little more leisurely," he explains. "And I try to jog two miles each day."

With this spiritual regimen undergirding him, Billy Graham constantly ventures forth into the world to preach his message—and his achievements have been recognized and applauded far beyond the bounds of his Christian faith. For example, in 1982 he was named the tenth recipient of the interfaith Templeton Prize for Progress in Religion and was awarded more than two hundred thousand dollars in recognition of his work. At the formal announcement of the award at the United Nations in New York City, Rabbi Marc Tanenbaum of the American Jewish Committee called Graham the greatest friend of the Jewish people in the twentieth century.

Yet, despite his position of honor and respect among people of many different religions, Graham tries never to compromise his simple Gospel message. In fact, he believes that the very reason for his success is that his basic message has remained unchanged since he began his ministry.

"The more one travels, the more one becomes interested in social issues," Graham says. And he has noted in no uncertain terms on many different platforms that he favors such issues as racial equality and a de-escalation of the nuclear arms race. "But even though there are a great many issues I am concerned about," he continues, "the main thrust of my message is exactly the same as it was thirty-five years ago. There's only one Gospel: the cross, and the resurrection of Christ, and our response to God's offer of forgiveness."

Finally, if Graham himself had to name one thing, what would he consider his greatest contribution to progress in religion?

For many people, the answer would lie in his ability to bring the Word of God to huge groups of people in mass meetings in stadiums—through smoothly produced television programs; through his many best-selling books; and in the widely circulated publications of the Billy Graham Evangelistic Association, such as *Decision* magazine.

But Graham sees things from a somewhat different perspective: "In God's eyes, I think that the most significant thing that I do is to worship Him. I think that worship is what He is pleased with more than anything else. It's what Mary was doing while Martha was tending to the dishes [Luke 10:38–42]. Both activities were important, but Jesus said of Mary, she's chosen the most important thing."

Graham, also, has always tried to choose "the most important thing" by tending first to his personal relationship with God. And his clear-cut sense of spiritual priorities in his private life seems to have been crucial in helping him accomplish great things in his public ministry as well.

Conclusion

These ten Templeton Prize recipients are just the first in what will likely be a long line of individuals who will be recognized by the Templeton Foundation for their contributions to progress in religion. The various judges for the prize will continue to ask themselves in the future, as they have in the past, three basic questions which set the tone for the award:

• What did this person do that was entirely original?

• Was that original achievement of a *spiritual* nature, rather than more generally humanitarian?

• Did this new thing result in a great increase in man's love of God or man's understanding of God?

Of course, reasonable men and women will disagree as to what constitutes an "original" spiritual development—or for that matter, whether it's even possible to have something entirely original. Also, they will have varying interpretations and definitions of what is "spiritual" and what is not. Finally there will certainly be different views of who God is and how one can establish an encounter with Him.

But the great vision and the high standards are there—to seek the original, the spiritual, and the love and understanding of God. If the caldron of religious competition, which too often boils over into misunderstanding and strife, can be controlled to any degree through efforts such as this award, great good rather than evil might be the result in our spiritually divided world.

Again, as Templeton himself has emphasized on many occasions, the goal for the Templeton Prize as well as other such interfaith efforts should not be syncretism, or the combining of all religions into one. No one should expect or be asked to take a position or engage in an action which would dilute or destroy his key beliefs. Rather, the ultimate aim should be an open consideration of the strengths of every faith and a willingness at least to *consider* incorporating a part of those strengths into one's own—without compromising basic tenets of doctrine and conviction.

Too often fears and misunderstandings have caused adherents of one faith to allow a particular religious or scientific technique or discovery to be appropriated entirely by another belief system— simply because that approach is held by those who believe differently. This is a shame, since that very technique or discovery might very well enrich the spiritual experience of the very individual who is so assiduously avoiding those who hold different convictions.

The ten Templeton Prize winners are among the best examples of how those who have taken great spiritual strides can teach important lessons about the outer limits of spirituality to those of other faiths. If future recipients can inspire deep thought, conviction, and action, as those of the past have done, John Templeton's dream of a continuing focus on progress in religion may indeed become reality.

About the Author

William Proctor, a graduate of Harvard College and Law School, is a full-time writer with many books to his credit. He is a sought-after collaborator and has coauthored *Adventures in Immortality* with George Gallup, Jr., and *The Return of the Star of Bethlehem* with Kenneth Boa.